Adverse Childhood Experiences, Adult Trauma, and the Return to Wholeness

Reflections and Tools for the Journey

Jane Buchan

Winter Blooms

Ontario & Vermont

ISBN 978-1-896760-05-6

Cover Design and Interior Typesetting by
FOGLIO | CUSTOM BOOK SPECIALISTS
Body set in *EB Garamond Regular 12pt*
Titles set in *Trade Gothic Next LT Pro Regular 17pt*

FOGLIOPRINT.COM

For Julie and her Return to Wholeness

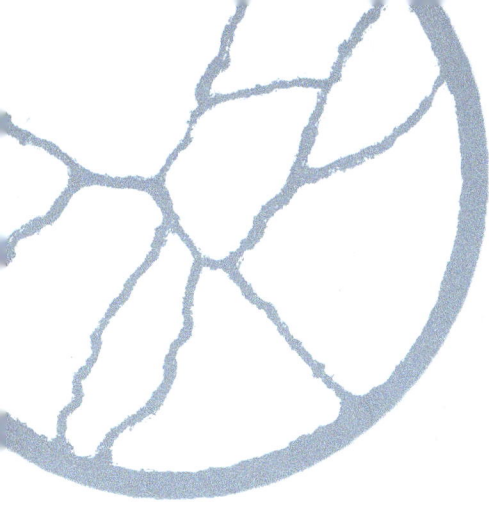

Author's Introduction

I have written this support booklet for folks living in the trauma trenches long enough to have experienced the stubborn reactivity of unhealed childhood wounds and the persistence of adult traumatic experiences months and years after the actual events occurred. For many of us (I too am a member of this vast Community of Souls; see the Appendixes for more about my personal trauma experiences.), life has had its challenges because of the usual suspects: emotional and/or physical abuse, and/or learning challenges, and/or disabilities, and/or bullies, and/or poverty, and/or racism, and/or gender violence, and, always, the cruelty of ignorant people. I say ignorant rather than evil because the word evil carries so much baggage. Generally, cruel people would do better if they knew better – wouldn't we all. Ignorance is something we can identify and remedy. I, you, we, can recognize ignorance by admitting when we feel lost and confused and angry for no apparent reason. When we take action to learn, to address our ignorance, we empower ourselves and are more understanding of others. All actions leading to compassion for ourselves and empathy for others are manifestations of our return to wholeness after traumas early and late.

Why do I say return to wholeness? I use the word *return* because, no matter the circumstances of our conception and birth, we are all born whole – that is, we are born as we are called into this world. At no other time in our history on this beautiful planet is our return to wholeness more important than now. The crises we are facing require the participation of every one of us. Since traumas often leave us feeling irreparably broken, we doubt our ability to make any kind of change in the larger world. We feel sidelined by our personal traumas, entirely depleted, and left with nothing we might give to or do for others. I created this booklet to help people who feel marginalized by trauma and its aftereffects learn practical techniques to support their return to wholeness.

We are each unique in our wholeness and at the same time we are all threads in the Web of Life on Earth. On the other side of our traumatic isolation is a world in need of our contributions to its repair and restoration. It is important that we know we are not alone in our suffering. It is also important that we know our return to wholeness will replace isolation with connections so rich and varied we will experience what it is to be *transformed*.

Jane Buchan, Winter, 2025

Adverse Childhood Experiences, Adult Trauma, and the Return to Wholeness

Reflections and Tools for the Journey

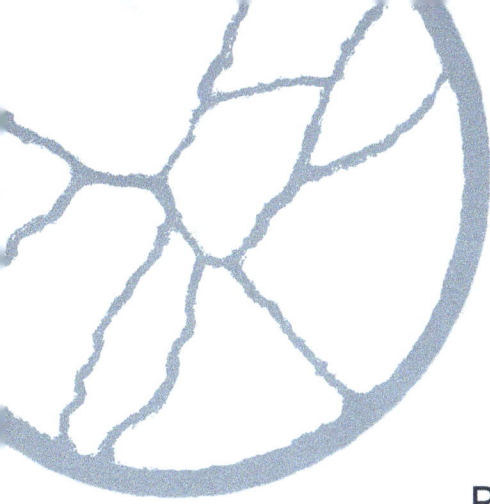

PART ONE

Returning to Wholeness

TRAUMA AND ISOLATION

Despite traumatic events beyond our control, we have survived and made our way to this moment. At times, we may feel proud of surviving, and at the same time feel a longing for something elusive, something we sense as unique to us, something precious. We feel discomfort if we talk about this longing because it is intensely personal. Everyone suffers, we tell ourselves. Suffering is an undeniable aspect of what our poets and mystics have called the Human Condition.

As well as our secret longing, we also feel trapped in our traumatic experiences. They make us feel vulnerable, and when we are criticized for "wallowing" in the past, we feel defensive. We say, "but you have no idea what this is like," and if we do not say these words aloud, we think them. Whenever we defend our preoccupations with trauma's influence in our lives, we burrow deeper into isolation, trauma's biggest challenge. To dismantle this sense of isolation, it helps to ask:

"What am I, are we, isolated from?"

We all have various answers to this question: We are isolated from loved ones. We are isolated from safety. We are isolated from trust. We are isolated from any belief system we had in a Benign Being who cares about us. We are isolated from the creature comforts we enjoyed before our traumatic experiences. We are isolated from the trustworthiness of our bodies, our intuition, our emotional connections, our joy. And we are isolated from this thing we secretly long for, this something that is unique and precious and mysterious.

This indescribable something is our wholeness.

Most people living with childhood and/or adult trauma feel isolated because we do not receive the immediate attention that would return us to safety and trust, that is, our wholeness, immediately after trauma. Doctors may repair our bodies, but they cannot repair our souls. Because trauma always requires outside intervention if we are to heal, interventions that are compassionate, understanding, soothing, and assuring, it is not enough to dress a physical wound and send us on our way. We must receive the emotional and spiritual wholeness of others through their expressions of care and concern to return us to our own wholeness. When we do not receive this care and concern, we become isolated in the traumatic aftermath of our experiences.

ISOLATION WHEN WE ARE YOUNG

Isolation is especially persistent when we endure trauma as children. At the beginning of our life journey, we lack the ability to understand the chaos of feelings and experiences we live with when we are hurt by those entrusted with our care. Without the inner resources to work through fear and despair, we feel captured by our traumatic reactivity. Our personal inner resources can only come to full flowering through our safe and loving relationships with adults who help us to name and express our traumas. Skilled adults do this through play, cuddling, daytime and bedtime stories, and, most important, recognition of and empathy for our suffering.

When we are received by empathetic and trustworthy people after trauma, we return to centre and the sense of wholeness temporarily eclipsed by trauma. Simultaneously, we learn how to comfort and care for ourselves in the present, adding to these skills as we grow older. The sad truth is, very few of us receive what we need to heal from trauma when we are young. Without the support of caring and skilled adults, our physical, emotional, intellectual, and spiritual reactivity becomes our first line of defense in situations that feel threatening. Think of a traumatized toddler's manic hyperactivity or deathly stillness and apparent lack of emotion after trauma. No matter our age at the time of trauma, we all experience this same state of shocking isolation.

Early childhood traumas are compounded by the inner and outer resource deficits natural to all babies, toddlers, and young children. The human brain is not built for trauma processing without support and this is especially true of young, developing brains. As well, in chaotic, unsafe childhood homes, these environments provide few, if any, positive human connections that are steady, trustworthy, and comforting.

Many people shy away from admitting they lacked adult support when they were young because such admissions suggest we had bad parents and guardians we feel we must protect in order to protect ourselves. Many traumatized babies and young children have parents who also suffered as children. This mutual suffering of child and parent establishes an intuitive emotional resonance that means children will automatically feel what their parents are experiencing even when parents are numb to their own experiences of trauma.

Describing parents as immature and unskilled does not violate the protectiveness we feel toward them. Most parents do not mean to let their children down; they simply are too preoccupied with their own challenges to provide comfort and safety to anyone else. Looking at our parents through a less judgmental lens creates the space to explore the worst that has happened to us with the intention of healing rather than attacking. Attacking our care-providers instills feelings of victimization, and no one wants to feel like a victim as we mature into authentic adulthood. Still, we have to admit the very hard truth: our parents let us down. When we most needed their comfort and wisdom, we didn't receive it.

ISOLATION WHEN WE ARE ADULTS

Those of us traumatized as adults experience this same sense of isolation, but in relation to the larger world. Religious people can feel deserted by the Being to whom they entrusted their safety; soldiers can feel betrayed by the governments they serve; natural disaster survivors can feel a crippling loss of trust in themselves and their communities; and, climate-crises survivors can lose faith in the goodness of life on Earth. Our peers and medical-team members may do their best to assure us we are fine, but if we have lost all trust in what before seemed so reliable we no longer stand on firm ground. In the time immediately following trauma, we are beyond solace, beyond comfort, beyond all the familiar sources of meaningful connection. Whether we are traumatized as children or as adults, we feel frighteningly alone.

The connecting bridge between traumatized children and adults is that children cannot begin to address their traumas until they are mature enough to do so. This means that traumatized adults, including adults traumatized as children, are also likely to experience resonant emotional connections with one another. War veterans feel for battered women; battered women feel for abandoned children; abused children often become members of their professional care communities when they are older, as personal support workers, firefighters, social workers, and therapists. Adults who have experienced childhood or adult traumas often feel a special bond with all marginalized people. We give money to homeless people, volunteer in soup kitchens, and find ways to serve vulnerable populations professionally because our personal traumas resonate with theirs. In this way, our traumas are connectors on an emotional level, transcending our personal isolation when we comfort others whose suffering touches our own.

TRAUMATIC ISOLATION, REACTIVITY, AND THE BIRTH OF DESPAIR

While isolation is common to all traumatized people, whether infants, toddlers, children, or adults, this isolation is often disguised by our determination to convince ourselves of our recovery from whatever has happened to us. Our insistence upon our recovery is a reliable defense against further vulnerability. It keeps the world out while it seals us in a hard shell that is intended to stifle our recurring terrors. We do not isolate ourselves intentionally, but automatically, for it is in our deepest traumatizing experiences that our autonomic nervous system takes over the role of adult care, in the case of children, and the role of trusted belief system, in the case of adults. Whether we are traumatized as children or adults, we flee reactively or fight wildly against all perceived threats. And when we can do neither, we disappear into the nothingness of dissociation, the autonomic, automatic internal shutting down that protects the traumatized through numbness.

Traumatized children have not lived long enough to develop healthy inner defenses and self-regulation skills that return us to safety. When early trauma remains unhealed because we lack safe and caring adult support, the time and energy we would otherwise invest in play that expresses our wholeness in pleasurable, inventive activities is diverted to manage survival crises. These crises ensure we become very good at enduring challenging, even brutal experiences. We make great first responders as adults, great soldiers, and great endurance-sports participants because high-stress activities make use of our trauma reactivity, especially our hypervigilance. We also become great at enduring horrific treatment from partners, institutions, and politicians. As traumatized children, because we are constantly on guard, we instinctively block opportunities for friendship and praise and are suspicious of kindness. We also become very good at engaging in conflicts that are exhausting yet familiar and therefore comforting. All these experiences normalize our isolation and despair.

Isolation in adults who experience trauma manifests similarly, but because of adult agency, we can disguise the isolation we feel, even from ourselves. However, we know in our bones that everything has changed and that because of the shocking, unpreventable, irreversible event we experienced, our sense of self, our ballast, is gone. To make up for this loss of comfort and stability, we search for ways to make sense of our new reality. Soldiers, for example, meet at the legion or rifle range or gym to forget what happened among those with whom their trauma wounds resonate, swinging between remembering and forgetting through wild camaraderie and numbing alcohol, drugs, and compulsive activity.

Only fellow battle survivors understand the pull to forget and to remember simultaneously. Domestic-abuse survivors also experience these isolating contradictions, as do all extreme-weather event and climate-crises survivors. After all such events, the world we have known is gone and we find ourselves in an existential hell where meaning is lost to us. We doubt the goodness of life. We search and search, but we cannot find any comfort in this new reality. We may try drugs, alcohol, food, sex, and other numbing activities, but their comfort is fickle, temporary, and potentially life threatening when used to excess. It is when we are deep in this profound despair that our longing to return to wholeness is born.

DESPAIR, ISOLATION, AND THE LOSS OF WHOLENESS

When trauma invades a child's daily life, little time is left for kid things like daydreaming, playing full out with curiosity, singing and dancing for joy, and jumping into experiences that reveal natural talents and inclinations. In fact, when children feel unsafe for a good part of every day, these positive activities may seem pointless because they don't require instinctive, survival-mode hypervigilance. As surviving siphons off the majority of our strength, the longing for wholeness kicks in. We cannot know until we begin our healing process that we are longing for the innocence, joy, and delight of our own lost childhood. We remain in this state of ignorance until we grow into more resourceful versions of ourselves and find supports for safely uncovering, expressing, and releasing our isolating pain.

For those who experience trauma as adults, we know only that we are suddenly isolated from the lives we have been creating through our resources and values. In this isolating aftermath, we cannot know why such life-destroying events happen specifically to us, and this inability to understand fills us with an anguish that can morph into rage in a moment. At these times, we look around for someone to blame. And then we attack ourselves, convinced we have done something to deserve the incalculable losses of safety and belonging. We also wonder if we'll ever trust again, if we'll ever smile or laugh again, if we'll ever experience the comfort of ordinary routine. We wonder, too, if we'll recover our sense of sure-footedness or if a part of us will always be off balance and waiting for the next explosion, the next sexual predator, the next car crash, the next hurricane, tornado, fire, flood, blizzard, earthquake. It is in this state of isolation that so many of us consider dying.

TRAUMA, SUICIDAL IDEATION, AND COMMUNITY

There is no one-size-fits-all remedy for suicidal ideation. For many trauma survivors, the pull to die becomes a common companion, often as strong as the longing for lost wholeness. Each of us must struggle with the pull to live and the pull to die, seeking help for this struggle every step of the way. Many of us find what we need in therapy's trust building processes. In therapy, we create safe space with another person and in that space, we safely name and express our despair. Slowly, our suicidal thoughts are replaced by the caring responses of this person with whom we are building trust.

In helping us to identify and express the pain we are in, many therapists and counsellors introduce us to the stories of others who have experienced traumas similar to our own. Women rocked by breast cancer diagnoses may learn for the first time of Dragon Boat Races for survivors. People struggling with eating, drug, and alcohol use may discover twelve-step programs that end their isolation through community. When we discover others have suffered and are suffering as we suffer, something our resonance with others has shown us all along, we are lifted out of isolation intellectually and emotionally and into a community of support that nurtures us as it invites our nurturing of others.

For trauma survivors, moving beyond their resonant connection to other survivors into intellectual and emotional connections can lead to deep personal understanding that adds spiritual meaning to our experiences. While we may feel set apart by our traumas, community relationships reveal a deeper level of what it means to be whole, to be human. In the company of those similarly traumatized, we return to the sense of belonging and community at our own pace and in our own time. In community, we rediscover our ability to trust others as we validate our own trustworthiness. We do this when we feel safe enough to experience and express our grief.

GRIEVING AND THE RETURN TO WHOLENESS

Like old age, grieving is not for sissies. Before we feel safe enough to grieve, we experience reactive energies that are very challenging to control whenever we feel unsafe. One of the great benefits of joining a community of trauma survivors comes with sharing and therefore normalizing the grieving process.

Processing what we are grieving is artful work. Sometimes the process starts with dismantling our anger and rage in the presence of empathetic witnesses. Sometimes we are flooded with emotions that take some time to regulate and identify. Every grieving process is unique. In the end, after we've weathered this process's storms and deathly calms, we share one thing. We share the empowerment we feel as we get to know our whole, unique, post-trauma selves.

Our post-trauma life is a journey of discovery, and, like all journeys, it requires planning and preparation. There are many tools to support our return to wholeness, and many ways to use these tools. One thing, however, is common to all of them. We must learn to use these tools ourselves.

Becoming competent at emotional self-regulation is as important as becoming competent in our professional lives. Competence through skill building leads to a sense of accomplishment that is deeply rewarding because these emotional and intellectual skills increase our sense of safety and our ability to reconnect with others.

No matter where our personal and professional post-trauma journeys may lead, all survivors of trauma must learn how to return to safety if we are to reconnect with others after triggering events.

What follows are tools that support our return to wholeness. They cost nothing but the time and commitment to learn them. Best of all, we all carry these with us into every situation in every moment of the day and night. While they are deceptively easy to master, they are also very easy to misplace when we become dysregulated. Learning to use these tools, practising them daily, and implementing them whenever we feel unsafe is evidence of our power and ingenuity, in short, our wholeness. Wholeness is our birthright, and returning to wholeness after trauma is a profoundly satisfying experience. Sharing our wholeness after its return connects us with others in joy, in sorrow, in trust, in hope, and in the eagerness to contribute to solving our shared personal, social, environmental, and political challenges.

NOTES

NOTES

NOTES

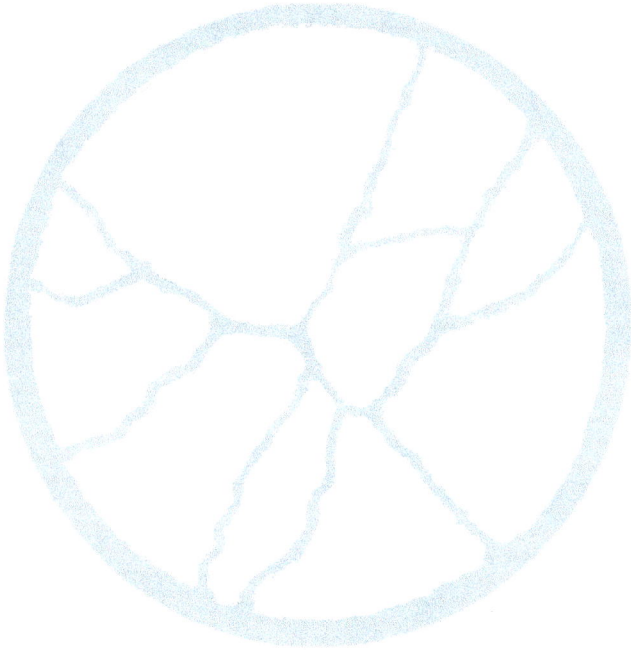

NOTES

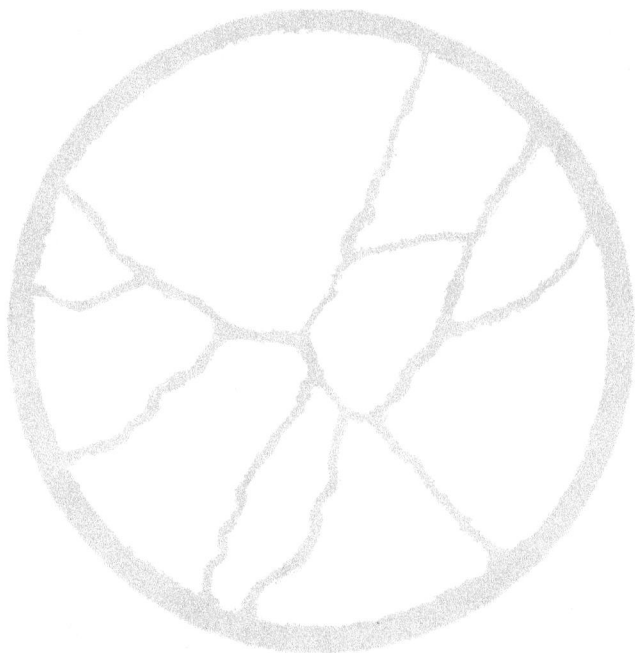

PART TWO

Tools for Safely Returning to Wholeness

E very challenging journey we undertake relies upon safety supports, and our return to wholeness after trauma is no exception. Naming and exploring our unhealed trauma wounds can be overwhelming because it is for the most part solitary work requiring the heart, the mind, the body, and the spirit to be fully present to past hurts. While individuals and caring communities can support us by listening to our discoveries without judgment and witnessing and validating our grief, no one can return to our earliest wounds for us.

These wounds are as unique as our finger prints and our nervous systems. They infect our bodies in much the same way that bacteria cause physical inflammation and illness. Rather than infections, we call the reactivity caused by trauma dysregulation. Learning how to self-regulate is absolutely essential before we begin our trauma excavations.

THREE PRIMARY SELF-REGULATION TOOLS

The most essential tools this sensitive work requires are present and ready for use in each of us. These self-regulation tools are **our awareness, our breathing, and our embodiment.** When used daily, these tools end our isolation and support our return to wholeness.

TOOL ONE: THE MIND/AWARENESS

Sometimes called mindfulness and linked to sitting meditation, awareness in its purest form requires no special training or skill to activate it beyond asking a simple question:

"What is happening right now?"

This question pulls us out of traumatic reactivity into the present moment with curiosity rather than fear. Sometimes the answer to this question takes a while to reveal itself, but with patience, we will receive an answer. We might discover a surprising insight such as, "I don't understand the look on that person's face," or, "I feel so empty I'm afraid I'll die," or, "I'm afraid of this place and I don't know why." Whatever the initial answer, it is a signal to shift to the next essential tool.

TOOL TWO: THE BREATH/AWARENESS

Because the hypervigilance caused by unhealed trauma negatively impacts our ability to remain present and calm, our nervous system is always focusing on danger, even when, for others, there is no danger. One manifestation of hypervigilance is the fight or flight reactivity that prepares us to defend ourselves or run away. A second manifestation of hypervigilance is the freeze reactivity that uses deathly stillness to return us to safety. These reactions to real or perceived threats are automatic, that is, involuntary; at a gut level the sympathetic nervous system is doing what it can to maintain safety, either by mobilizing us to take action through fighting or escaping, or by shutting us down through a process called dissociation. All three reactions – fighting, fleeing, and freezing – can affect our breathing in two very significant ways.

Hyperventilation, the shallow rapid breathing that announces a **panic attack**, is the most noticeable of these breathing alterations. Because panic attacks are visible to others, they are an automatic means of attracting help. In ideal circumstances, the people around us notice we are flushed or pale, agitated, or wild eyed. These folks come to our rescue with paper bags for us breathe into to reduce our over-oxygenated blood by breathing and rebreathing the bag's CO_2 saturated air. If they know us well enough, they offer soothing back rubs to calm us. Generally, hyperventilating inspires the actions of others to support our return to safety.

A subtler trauma reaction is **breath holding**, another automatic reaction that can lead to anoxia, an oxygen deprivation state that induces the protective deep-freeze state we call dissociation. When we dissociate our awareness shuts down. This state does the opposite of hyperventilation. It renders us numb to ourselves and invisible to others. We do our best to disappear because in traumatizing environments at least, being noticed often means being attacked in some way.

Both hyperventilating and breath holding are every traumatized person's automatic/autonomic means of defending against actual and perceived threats. Once we are aware of when and how we hyperventilate or hold our breath, asking "what is going on right now?" will include awareness of our breathing. When we are aware of our breathing, we can develop the skills to replace hyperventilation and breath holding with self-regulating breathing that will return our sense of safety.

TOOL THREE: THE BODY/AWARENESS

In the best of circumstances, our life experiences cultivate a sense of physical pleasure, strength, and ingenuity. Our physical bodies are the expression of our total existence, including that which is visible to the naked eye and that which is invisible. An embodied person is capable of being fully present to themselves and others, not only physically, but emotionally, intellectually, and spiritually. When we experience unpreventable, frightening events without immediate after-care interventions, traumatic reactivity takes over the work of keeping us safe. When this happens, we no longer trust ourselves and escape our flesh and the situation through dissociation.

RETURNING TO SAFETY: REGULATING OUR BREATHING

Awareness of how we are breathing supports our safety because, as we learn very early, breathing is essential to life. When we breathe deeply, with long, slow exhales through the mouth, we are initiating the first line of defense against both panic and dissociation. Learning to regulate our breathing is very helpful for people healing from trauma because it breaks the patterns of fighting, fleeing, and freezing.

Deep, slow breathing also grounds us in the present moment. In any stressful, triggering circumstance, consciously altering our breathing allows us to identify with our resourced, adult self, identification that supports our safety. What follows is a simple action plan to self-regulate by becoming aware of our breathing and regulating our breaths.

SELF-REGULATED BREATHING ACTION PLAN

1. Place both hand on your belly, that is, the area below your waist.

2. Take a deep belly breath **in through the nose** for a count of six as you imagine the breath traveling down into your belly to "meet" your hands.

3. Release this breath **through the mouth** with a quiet "woo" sound for a longer count, helping the exhalation with the very slight pressure of your hands on your belly.

4. Repeat this pattern at least three times.

5. Use this breathing pattern before meetings, to refresh yourself when you're feeling drained or worried, and whenever you want to cultivate mental clarity after an unsettling incident that triggers the question, "What is going on here?"

Employ self-regulated breathing before you share your unsettling experience with anyone else. Regulating breath work is **empowering** because we learn that our own actions can restore us to safety. Self-regulated breathing also fosters **self-efficacy**, the inner knowing that we can solve problems and accomplish our goals even after many failed attempts to do so.

Put another way, the self-regulating breath work described above creates opportunities to experience our ability to make positive changes. When we embrace this ability – and our need – to create a resourceful response to replace an automatic reaction, we are reconnecting with our competence and resourcefulness. After trauma and before we develop self-regulating techniques, we search for others outside ourselves for support.

While this outside support comforts, it should not replace our intention to become confident, strong, self-regulating adults. Always searching for someone else to support us in times of traumatic reactivity is exhausting and makes us feel incompetent, helpless, and even childish. Learning to regulate our breathing effectively and practising this technique in a variety of situations helps us to avoid forming toxic co-dependent relationships tainted by the unspoken agreement that we agree to be weak in order for others to feel strong.

Talking with a friend after we have self-regulated is a great thing to do if it feels right. In friendships, we meet as equals, with both people participating in the give and take of expressing thoughts and feelings. In these relationships, we open our hearts, share our secrets, and inspire one another. True friendships empower and inspire both people. Pseudo-friendships, what Cheryl Richardson calls arrangements, are great for superficial connections, but they can actually impede deep sharing and personal growth.

AWARENESS, GROUNDING, AND EMBODIMENT

Once we are aware of our breathing and employ the self-regulating breathing techniques that return us to safety, we are ready to expand our safety by **grounding ourselves in the present moment.** We do this by shifting our awareness to the details of our immediate physical environment. One way to do this is through a **visual scan.**

For example, you can choose to become aware of three to five items in your immediate surroundings. This awareness takes the form of naming items, such as "my brown boots," "that red chair," or "the black car." **By focusing on what we see in the present moment, we initiate the grounding process.** Just as the breath we hold is expelled by regulated breathing, so the blind terror or rage we feel when triggered is replaced by the comforting familiarity of ordinary, everyday items in our environment.

We accelerate this grounding process by shifting our attention from our immediate environment to the body. Becoming aware of the soles of our feet, the sensation of opening and closing our hands, and/or bouncing subtly all help to root us in the present moment and in the body. **These strategies continue to feed our empowerment – our experience of taking action in the world – and our sense of self-efficacy – the belief that we can endure and overcome many failures in the pursuit of our goals. Both empowerment and self-efficacy are essential supports in our return to wholeness.**

When practiced regularly, these powerful skills become habits that prove our competence, our resourcefulness, and our ability to recover from challenges and move forward. Empowerment and self-efficacy also prove our courage. **Courage is always present when we choose to learn how to return to safety while experiencing traumatic reactivity.**

GROUNDING IN THE PRESENT ACTION PLAN

1. Look around the setting you are in to become aware of the colour and size of something close, such as "this large brown desk in front of me." Touch your thumbs to your forefingers as you notice your object.

2. Find another object in the setting that is a little farther away, such as "the white ceiling overhead." Touch your thumbs to your middle fingers as you notice this second object.

3. Find a third object that you're wearing, such as "my flat black boots," or whatever you're wearing on your feet. Touch your thumbs to your ring fingers as you notice your third object.

4.   Find a fourth object farther away, such as "that light or window or window shade on the far side of the room." Touch your thumbs to your baby fingers as you notice your fourth object.

5.   Find your original object and move from it to the second, the third, and the fourth; repeat them in or out of order as you look at each one and breathe in through the nose and out through the mouth with a slightly longer exhale. For this final review, clench and unclench your fists to stretch the tendons of your hands.

USING OUR HANDS TO GROUND AND EMBODY

For most people, our hands are one of the earliest means of discovering the world. Even as very young infants, we touch things, taste them, pick at our clothes, reach for a toy. In doing so, we discover the connecting power of our hands. The human will to explore and discover is obvious during and after birth and an early expression of our wholeness. Ideally, we labour our way through the birth canal in partnership with our mother. Once in the world, our hands gravitate to breast or bottle during our very first feeding.

If we're fortunate, we have working hands throughout our lives. As children, we learn to finger paint and hold crayons. We mature into performing more complicated tasks such as doing up buttons and zippers and brushing our teeth. As we mature, we learn to use our hands to master increasingly complex tasks, thinking nothing about these accomplishments after a time, and taking our skills for granted.

Most of us master many skills when we are quite young. Long before we step onto the playing fields of elementary school, we learn to roll and throw and kick a ball. As we grow older, depending upon what we witness around us, we learn to touch lovingly or we learn to harm with our hands. We bring our hands to our faces as we think or study. We stroke or twist our hair with our hands to self soothe during tests. Instinctively, our hands spring into defensive action to protect us when we trip.

Our hands are vitally important to our sense of safety. They are also easier to work with in public than any other part of the body. Become aware of your hands throughout your days and nights. Love and appreciate them. Relate to them as guardians and protectors as well as useful body parts. Take good care of your hands. Keep them clean and protected from heat and cold. When working with sharp objects, protect them with work gloves. As you prepare for bed, think of all the ways your hands connect you to others and to the tasks you perform throughout the day. Place them over the centre of your chest with gratitude before you fall asleep. When you awaken in the night, become aware of your hands. Open them if they are clenched. If you sleep on your side, bring them into prayer position by your face for a few seconds.

By using our hands to perform skills and techniques that support self-regulation, we increase our confidence in our ability to care for ourselves. Returning to centre after a triggering episode is empowering because awareness, regulated breathing, and grounding/embodying techniques during potential and actual reactivity increase our confidence in our adult resourcefulness. After several applications of these tools, our growing sense of self-efficacy, that internal knowing that we have overcome serious obstacles in the past and can do so in the future, supports our desire to solve all sorts of problems.

MORE ABOUT EMPOWERMENT AND SELF-EFFICACY

Both empowerment and self-efficacy build over time. **Empowerment** teaches us to look outward, to discern, often from others, what tools are useful to add to our self-regulation tool kit. We find support online in videos offering demonstrations of techniques that address anxiety through stretching, acupressure massage, and other comforting actions. We also find support in our therapy sessions when a therapist teaches practical ways to successfully navigate specific challenges. Self-help books are also a source of empowerment tips and, as a bonus, build a sense of community. Not only do we learn valuable techniques from these works, we also learn that whatever we're experiencing is a shared human experience, an expression of the Human Condition. Reading these books reminds us that everyone has a story, and that everyone suffers. If this weren't the case, such books would not exist. In fact, connecting members of my ACEs and adult-trauma community is why I wrote this one.

Self-efficacy is, by contrast, an inside job. It increases through many attempts – and failures – to reach a goal. Smoking cessation offers a great example of the self-efficacy building process. Many begin with the cold-turkey approach. Willpower works for a while, but if we haven't addressed our reasons for smoking, we go back to it again and again, often after years of not smoking. During those early non-smoking periods, we never really lose the urge to smoke.

After struggling for years, quitting and relapsing over and over again, we find some empowering key offered by someone sharing their personal experiences along with the wisdom they gathered to support others in their intention to become non-smokers. It is our failures followed by renewed efforts to quit smoking that foster our sense of self-efficacy, that feeling that we can accomplish anything through persistence and the commitment to do so, regardless of the difficulty.

EMPOWERMENT, SELF-EFFICACY, AND THE PRESENT MOMENT

Becoming aware of our breathing, then of what we're wearing on our feet, the heaviness or lightness of our clothing, and the sensation of opening and closing our hands all help to root our attention in the present moment. This grounding work is itself empowering because it provides the lived experience of personal agency, that sense that we can take whatever action we need whenever a need for action arises. Pushing our feet into the floor or our hands against a wall or piece of furniture takes us out of the reactivity of a triggering experience and into the present's potential for support and safety. Saying or thinking, "I feel my hands on my thighs," or "I feel my feet connect with this floor," or "I am pushing my hands against this wall," interrupts the flow of reactive sensations with empowering, fresh, present-moment sensations and thoughts.

Our ability to replace traumatic reactivity with grounding sense experiences is essential to our feelings of competence, whether at home or out in the world. It is wise to remind ourselves often that the after-effects of traumatizing experiences manifest as a super-sensitive nervous system. Soothing our nervous system using self-regulating tools that are always available to us lessens the likelihood of emotional meltdowns or relapses into harmful behaviours to achieve a sense of safety. To support self-regulation by using these tools, it is good to remember that:

1. Learning and using the tools is empowering: "I know I can find what I need."

2. Employing grounding tools increases our self-efficacy: "I almost had a meltdown, but I returned to centre quickly and will likely come to centre even more quickly next time."

AN ALTERNATIVE GROUNDING ACTION PLAN

1. Bring your attention to your body, specifically to your breath. Slow your breathing down. If you're comforted by counting, count to six as you inhale through the nose and count to eight or ten as you exhale through your mouth. If you dislike counting, simply exhale through the mouth for as long as you can. Begin with three to five breaths with long, slow exhales.

2. Gently guide your attention to your hands. Note whether they are cold or warm, clammy or dry. Place them on your thighs. Feel their weight and temperature. Feel how they encourage your energy to flow down your legs and into the floor or ground.

3. Shift your attention to your feet. Wiggle your toes for a moment. Then gently pulse the balls of your feet against the floor, alternating left, then right, for a count of twenty, ten pulses for each foot.

4. Bring your attention to your shoulders and any tension you may be holding there. Subtly rotate them, first forward, then back, then forward again.

5. With a downward moving scan, slide your attention from your head and shoulders, to your chest, to your arms and hands, and finally to the lower half of your torso, slowly traveling from waist to pelvis to pubic bone to thighs, knees, calves, and ankles, then to the soles of your feet and your connection with the supports beneath them.

By employing awareness of our breathing and grounding in present-moment sights and sensations, we feel more empowered and increase our store of self-efficacy. With self-regulating tools always available to return us to safety should we feel traumatic reactivity, we are ready to explore any thoughts, feelings, and sensations that contradict our sense of wholeness. Knowing we can employ a tool to return to safety is a sign of growing resourcefulness. When we use the following tools, we increase our experience of the resourcefulness that helps us to recognize our wholeness.

NOTES

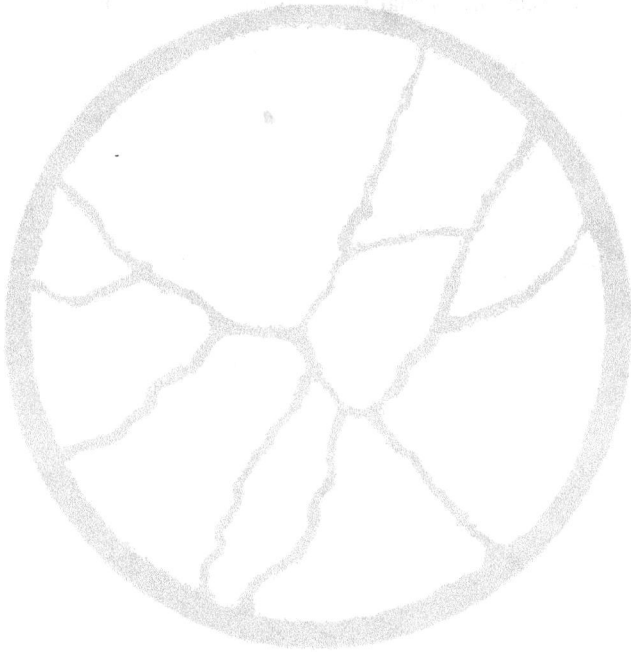

NOTES

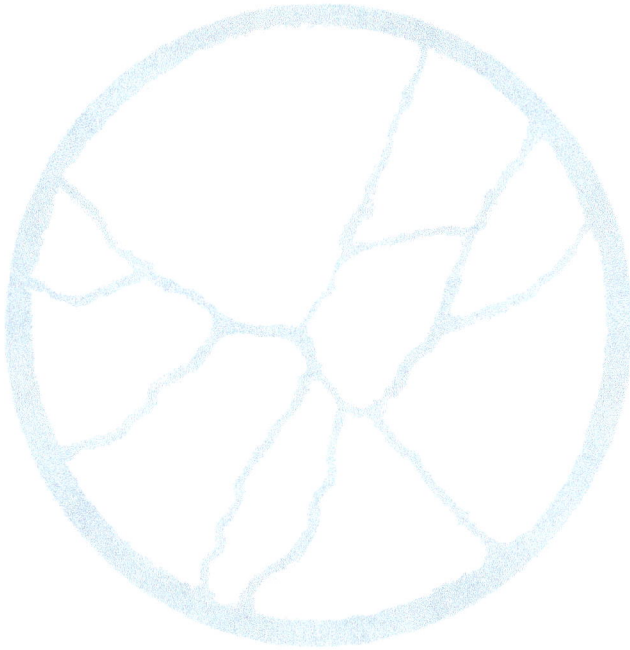

NOTES

NOTES

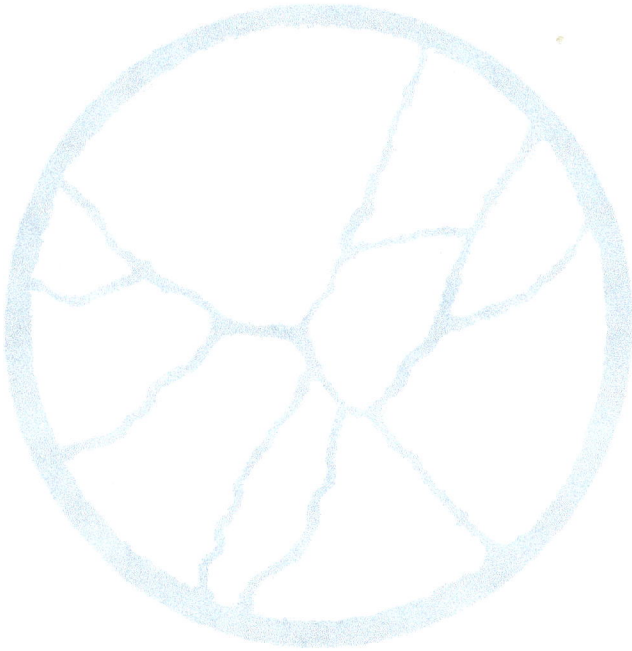

PART THREE

Safely Transforming Trauma-Generated Thoughts, Feelings, and Sensations

After we experience trauma, many of us ignore or fight against our feelings of incompetence, helplessness, and loss because they make us feel vulnerable. More often than not, our resistance to feeling these and trauma-caused thoughts and sensations increases their frequency and intensity. Fighting against them leaves us feeling depleted and defeated. To avoid this inner power struggle, it is helpful to create routines and habits that support turning our attention from external distractions to our inner life and our intention to return to wholeness.

Many of us are stumped by the idea of an inner life. We ask: "What inner life? My life's my life. No inner, no outer." Our inner and outer lives can appear indistinguishable until we become curious, not simply about our persistent reactivity, but about our inexplicable depressions, sudden anger flares, and furtive mean-spirited thoughts and acts.

Understanding our traumatic reactions requires that we become aware of where we place our attention throughout the day and night. When we look at **screens**, we are dominated by external stimulation that often prompts impulsive action such as shopping online after seeing popup ads, signing up for classes and seminars we do not need or want to take, and scrolling through endless posts that temporarily obliterate our desire to return to wholeness. Reactions to external cues dominate our lives until we make space to **cultivate** our inner reality.

Notice this word cultivate. It comes from the Latin verb *colere*, to till, to toil over, to care for. Cultivating our inner reality is very much like actual gardening. It requires the same daily dedication, in the case of our inner lives, to water with attention, to identify weedy, negative thoughts when they choke out our longing to return to wholeness, and to recognize our reactivity and calm these sensations with self-regulating actions. How do we become faithful stewards of our inner reality? We do it by making time and space for it in much the same way we create a physical space for a garden. Our inner life, strengthened through reflection, through pondering the circumstances in our lives with curiosity rather than judgment, pulses with responsive joy when we take the time to engage with it. Think of the joy we feel when we smile at a baby and the baby smiles back, of coming home to a beloved person or pet after an absence. This same joy sparks when we turn our attention inward, to the place where our wholeness patiently waits for our attention.

DEVELOPING THE HABIT OF REFLECTION

I first became aware of people's disconnection from their inner states when I taught literature and other humanities courses to college students. Many were in two-year programs designed to build skills for specific jobs. Most of these students were goal oriented, habituated to memorizing facts and repeating information on tests that required rote learning for successful completion. These courses required little if any critical thinking skills and were so fast-paced they crowded out any time for curiosity about the wisdom of using the information they were required to memorize. Answers were right or wrong. Complex issues were over-simplified into small chunks of data. To pass tests and exams, students had to repeat specific facts, theories, and applications without asking about their implications for the larger world. This data mining and memorization is the work of the left hemisphere of the brain.

By contrast, Humanities courses generally, and Literature courses specifically, employ both hemispheres of the brain, the left hemisphere for analysis and application, the right for experiencing the whole of a work of art. A simple explanation of the differences between STEM courses – Science, Technology, Engineering, and Mathematics – and "the Arts" – Literature, History, Philosophy, Classics and the like – is this: STEM courses quantify and measure to arrive at useful applications of information, while Humanities courses explore and reflect on the qualitative value of human and other-than-human life experiences. The differences between STEM and Humanities courses are complementary, providing balance between the qualitative, anecdotal awareness inspired by arts courses and the quantitative research-based methodologies that inform science, technology, engineering and math courses. Put in yet another way: STEM courses catalog data to increase our information while humanities courses explore and reflect on the deeper meaning of this information. William Bruce Cameron, author of *Informal Sociology*, captures this difference in his memorable, **"Not everything that can be counted counts, and not everything that counts can be counted."** (Random House, NY, 1963, p 13)

When we read a short story, there is no right answer to questions about the nature of character, the relevance of setting, and the significance of themes. All responses are welcomed as long as we point to something in the text that validates the connections we've made. Such answers require that we reflect on the **possible** meaning of a story's various moving parts to ground our perspectives in the writer's vision as expressed on the page. By contrast, a how-to manual about operating a computer must be about the mechanics of the technology rather than, say, reflections on the long-term consequences of the computer on human life and the world in which we live.

REFLECTION AND WHOLENESS

Those of us who feel safe and secure trust our physical, mental, emotional, and spiritual intelligences. We may not be conscious of these vast reservoirs of guidance, but the circumstances of our lives make it possible for us to trust ourselves to make good decisions and choices even in ambiguous situations. We tend to have good spatial awareness, healthy boundaries, and robust appetites for learning. We practice self-regulating behaviours like deep breathing and positive self-talk to bring us back to centre after a distressing experience. Sudden door slams, car back fires, or unexpected shouts may cause us to jump, but we quickly find our way back to the calm and present-moment peace that provide our sense of wholeness, that "I've got this" feeling and knowing.

As beloved children, we learn self-care habits from our parents. When we're overtired as toddlers and children, our care givers guide us into restful atmospheres. When we're angry, they encourage moderating behaviours such as counting clouds, having a drink of water, or dancing around until we are calm and can speak of what made us angry. When our blood sugar drops, we are encouraged to eat something nutritious. And, through all this loving attention, we are learning the habits of reflection because we are taught how to think and feel our way into our inner experiences and our regulated states.

When we are comforted out of our distress as children, we are, simultaneously, internalizing the processes of self-care and reflection. Physical and emotional comforts support learning, reflection, resilience, intimacy, and mutually satisfying social connections. We adopt these self-care skills naturally, because we learn from trusted adults how good they make us feel.

By contrast, adults who as children felt unsafe because we lacked trusted-adult guidance, often find ourselves in a constant state of dysregulation. We are hypervigilant, trapped in a high-alert state everyone should feel in the presence of real danger but one that unhealed traumatized folk experience most of the time. Many adults who were traumatized children find countless ordinary situations dangerous, including those that foster our mental and physical health such as sleeping, eating, and playing. Our nervous systems are always on guard and ready to fight, run away, or disappear into the protective cocoon of a dissociation state. No wonder trauma leaves little time for reflection. Trauma reactivity means every situation is potentially threatening, so of course scrolling through meaningless data is a safe way to pass time while waiting for the next and the next and the next jolt of reactive energy. Because of our high-alert orientation, we need skills that provide even more safety than the basics of awareness, regulated breathing, and embodied awareness.

MORE TOOLS FOR THE SAFE RETURN TO WHOLENESS

TOOL #1: ACTIVE IMAGINATION

Psychiatrists and psychologists often express differing opinions concerning how to move through rage into peace, sorrow into joy, discontent into contentment. In spite of their ideological differences, these specialists all share the core belief in the existence of our unconscious mind. Often called simply the unconscious or the shadow part of the self, the unconscious mind supports our healing by providing unexpected insights through dreams, meaningful chance events, and other apparently random experiences.

Carl Jung, one of the early explorers and cartographers of the unconscious, developed a simple method of communication with this shadowed aspect of the self. He called his method **Active Imagination**, a technique requiring we employ our imagination when asking this mysterious reservoir of guidance questions, then pausing to receive our answers. This process of asking and pausing for an answer strengthens our ability to reflect on our life circumstances. The steps for employing this method of communication with the unconscious are simple and yet supportive of the deepening reflections we need to expand our healing process. What follows are the steps to an easily accessible version of Carl Jung's Active Imagination protocol.

CONTACTING YOUR UNCONSCIOUS
THROUGH ACTIVE IMAGINATION

To begin, choose writing and drawing implements (pen, pencil, marker, paper). These can be items you find around your living space, or, you can make a specific investment in your Active Imagination explorations by buying new materials you dedicate to this task. Whether you find them or buy them, set aside these writing materials for this work. When you're not using them, put them away, along with any written reflections, in a private place.

GUIDELINES FOR SUCCESSFUL USE OF
JUNG'S ACTIVE IMAGINATION TECHNIQUE

First, if you don't already know how, it is time to learn to write in cursive. Do not hand print or use a computer or electronic tablet. Cursive writing strengthens the health of the whole brain by requiring the left and right hemispheres to work together in the Active Imagination reflection process. **Trauma isolates and fragments, forcing the left brain into active duty to promote safety through analysis and strict adherence to rules.** Obsessive-Compulsive-Disorder (OCD), for example, is often a shortcut to feelings of safety for survivors of trauma.

Cursive writing is very different because it creates a collaborative whole out of apparent unrelated bits and pieces. Many research studies have proven cursive writing supports trauma recovery. If you've never learned cursive, spend time at **consistentcursive.com**. Internet searches for other "learn-cursive" sites will provide other opportunities to learn and practice cursive writing before you begin your Active Imagination practice.

Don't worry. If you've never learned cursive writing, it won't take long to do so. Our handwriting is a unique expression of our individuality, a form of drawing that in calligraphy reaches the level of high art. As such, it is an indispensable tool in returning to wholeness which, after all, is the sum total of our individual unique parts and at the same time our ability to connect with and contribute to the greater whole we share with all species.

After you have written daily for several days, you'll notice its absence should you be prevented from taking up your pen. That sense of missing something vital is the Soul's prompting to re-member – re-member – yourself. Cursive writing is a tool for re-membering and expressing our wholeness. It lives on the page so we can revisit our wholeness discoveries again and again. If cursive is a new skill, it may take a little time to feel comfortable communicating this way. That is all right. Remember, self-efficacy is built over time and through failure after failure. If your letters look childish, that is just fine. The more we write in cursive, the more we discover its revelatory powers. No two letters are alike. Your goal is to learn to join them in a way that is understandable to you, and, if you wish, to others. Writing in cursive daily will form an amazing support in your return to wholeness.

ACTIVE IMAGINATION ACTION PLAN

Once you feel comfortable writing in cursive, follow these steps:

1. **Write a question with your dominant hand.** For example, you might write:

    a. How can I best heal from my trauma? or,

    b. What is preventing me from knowing how to move forward in my life? or,

    c. Where can I find peace and restore my sense of safety?

2. **Move the pen or pencil to your non-dominant hand and write the first thing that comes to you.** It may be a single word like "FEAR." It may be the sentence, "This is stupid." Notice the cursive writing with your non-dominant hand looks more childlike when compared to the question written with your dominant hand. This is an important difference. Your unconscious has shown up through your non-dominant hand and is eager to communicate with your conscious self as expressed by your dominant-hand writing.

Trust whatever comes; let your non-dominant hand scribble out mistakes, just the way children scribble out things they want to change. Then write more questions with your dominant hand.

Take your time. Let the process unfold as it will. One day, you will have a very clear idea of something very important to you that has been buried beneath traumatic reactivity. Perhaps it is the freedom to learn something, such as another language, or a skill, such as swimming. Perhaps it is the courage to tell your story to yourself in a memoir, or a short story, or novel that tells your story through an imagined character. Perhaps you want to paint or draw visions and dreams that have haunted you. Perhaps you want to return to school to learn a profession you would have pursued earlier had you not experienced trauma. Be faithful in your Active Imagination work. Practice it daily. Record your questions and answers as well as your insights, those sudden flashes of understanding and inspiration that come when we develop the habit of reflection. Draw any images that come forward for you to reflect upon. At some point, you'll have a clear idea, in writing, of something you truly long to do to mark or celebrate or confirm your return to wholeness.

Keep in mind, your unconscious is dreamlike AND realistic. You may think you want to be a professional ballerina, but if you are in your sixties without any dance experience and the skill, flexibility, and contacts to stage a comeback, your unconscious won't support this goal. If your previous experience does not include professional dance, your unconscious may translate your longing to be a ballerina into a single word such as "dance," or "studio."

When you see the words that describe the wholeness treasures buried in your unconscious, they will resonate in your heart with the force of a spiritual calling. One word or phrase will lead to another and another, and soon you'll be able to expand your Active Imagination relationship and refine other action steps on your return to wholeness. If the word "dance" becomes your guiding star, you might want to take tap lessons to support cardio health, or become a member of a dance studio offering expressive dance. Perhaps you'll want to create studio space for adults who want to explore trauma through dance. The more Active Imagination questions you ask with your dominant hand, and the more thoughts and images you record with your non-dominant hand, the more clarity you'll have for the next technique, one that strengthens the partnership with your unconscious mind, your intuition, and your powers of reflection.

TOOL #2: GRAPHIC STORYTELLING

Graphic Storytelling has taken hold of our culture through works like *Persepolis* and other graphic novels. Similar to cartooning, graphic writing uses images as well as words to tell a story. Words are sometimes lost to us when we are traumatized, and images tend to support our recovery of verbal expressions by showing us what we're as yet unable to express. This is why movies, documentaries, and TV shows contribute to trauma healing. They express stories that reflect our own, stories we are not yet able to tell.

Although Graphic Storytelling can be confused with Vision Boarding, there are significant differences. The primary difference is vision boarding's New Age focus on manifesting something concrete that people want but do not have. Graphic Storytelling is not about "getting" a partner or a new apartment or a better car, although we may attain these material items. Unlike this "getting" or "manifesting" intention, Graphic Storytelling's intention is to reveal some aspect of our wholeness we have temporarily lost to trauma.

Such stories reveal the completeness, the wholeness, we already possess but have lost touch with because of trauma. In its revelatory capacity, Graphic Storytelling restores what traumas steal: our relationships with and experiences of our wholeness. Images that we create and find in magazines or on the net can express emotionally and spiritually what is temporarily lost to us intellectually and physically.

GRAPHIC STORYTELLING ACTION PLAN

1. Graphic Storytelling can be done on a small or large scale. You can tell your story in a journal, on a white or cork board, or even on wall space. Wherever and however you choose to tell your story, make sure you have the space to tell it sequentially. In this space, we create a story with a beginning, a middle, and an end. Some people like to make frames, cartoon style. Others like a chapter approach such as we find in 'Once upon a time' fairy and folk tales.

2. Whether you create a booklet or a mural, make sure you have room for images expressing the feelings and thoughts you experience about what reflects or describes your wholeness. You can sketch or paint these images, choose magazine photos and drawings, or you can use a combination of found-and-created art to create your story.

3. Wherever and however you choose to tell your story, make sure all your images help you to reflect on being seen, display your courage and perseverance, and express your delight at returning to wholeness. Add to or replace images whenever you feel called to do so. When some image no longer expresses your journey authentically, tweak your story with updated images.

4. Allow your graphic story to transform until you feel it is complete. Trust that you'll find just the right images as you need them. When you feel stuck, ask "Now what?" The Listening Heart that is the Universe is always eager to be in partnership with us as we return to wholeness. Go through your story daily. Reflect on its contents throughout your days. At night, when ready for bed, ask to dream about your wholeness and how it might be expressed through your graphic storytelling.

Please note: Keep all electronics out of your sleeping space, or if they must be there, turn them off and cover them with beautiful cloth. Thrift stores always have lots of scarves to choose from. When you keep your electronics under wraps in your sleeping space, you support your very personal dream life, essential to your return to wholeness. We are all dreamers, whether we remember our dreams or not. Claim your rights as a dreamer by keeping electronics out of the sacred space dreaming requires to flourish.

TOOL #3: EMOTIONAL FREEDOM TECHNIQUES (EFT)

Engaging your mind, emotions, and spirit in the process of working with your unconscious supports the creativity at the heart of our wholeness. Engaging your physical self by tapping, massaging, and holding specific places on the body during reactivity connects with the stories this reactivity expresses. **All traumatic experiences express as reactivity – including sensations, pain, flashbacks, memories, hyperawareness, and hypervigilance – until we feel safe enough to invite these stories to reveal themselves.** Before our traumatic stories have a voice, they express as emotion, such as fear when we're exposed to unexpected, or loud noise. Sometimes reactivity expresses as dread and anxiety as when we find ourselves in ambiguous and therefore frightening situations. Sometimes this reactivity expresses as flashbacks – images of past violence triggered by a smell or a texture or the look on another's face – these images terrifying when they unpredictably explode out of the past into the present. War veterans are eloquent in their descriptions of how flashbacks take them out of the present moment and back into the horrors of battle. Traumatized children and adults who have survived domestic violence, car or plane crashes, and extreme weather events have similar sensory, shocking flashbacks.

Even when we are overwhelmed by flashbacks, when we touch the body with the intention to soothe and to heal, the body recognizes that the adult self is present and can be trusted to care for us in a way that our caregivers or comrades could not during the original, traumatizing event. The intention to connect as a caring adult when we are in the flashback creates a physical experience of safety. Repeated after the flashback, as when we reflect and write and feel our way into the past in the present moment as a resourceful adult, soothes the body as well as the intellect, emotions, and spirit. The ability and willingness to soothe ourselves out of traumatizing imagery is evidence of our return to wholeness.

The comfort we provide ourselves in the moment of a traumatic flashback rebuilds the self-trust lost to trauma. After such moments of soothing attention, we have actual experience of meeting our own needs and returning to safety. Self-trust and trust in others are among the first casualties of trauma. Reactivating trust in ourselves, even when we resist trusting others, is an empowering activity that fosters our courage to continue to do whatever we can to return to wholeness. Using body-inclusive techniques such as Emotional Freedom Techniques accelerates our healing by reestablishing this trust.

EMOTIONAL FREEDOM TECHNIQUES ACTION PLAN

1. Because our reactivity is so strong and its patterns so familiar, it is best to begin an EFT session by breathing slowly and deliberately as described in Part Two, with deep breaths in through the nose and long, slow exhales through the mouth.

2. To further support safety, place one hand on the centre of the chest and with the fingers of the other hand, massage the space between the tendons of the baby and ring fingers. (See the image below and visit winterblooms.net; click on the

EFT tab to learn more about this and other tapping points and how they connect to our organs, meridians, and vascular and nervous systems to clear the reactivity stored in them.)

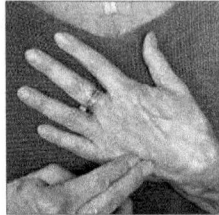

3. Massage this back-of-hand space when feeling fear, dread, anxiety, and hypervigilance. Massaging this space assures the body we are learning to care for ourselves by taming the reactivity that occurs in trauma's aftermath.

4. Begin your use of this somatic technique gently, for no more than a half an hour each day. Even ten or fifteen minutes can seem like an eternity at the beginning of your return to wholeness. For traumatized people, the stillness reflection requires can make us feel exposed and threatened, triggering the fight, flight, or freeze reactions designed to help us feel safe. Massaging this back-of-hand point, also called the Gamut Point because it has a broad range of uses, is a powerful self-regulating tool to add to your toolkit.

5. **It is wise to remind ourselves that using EFT to communicate with old wounds is a forgiving and artful process**. There is no need to "get anything right." We are learning to communicate with the body – our faithful story keeper and story spinner – in a way that is nurturing and healing. Gentleness is always best. Returning to wholeness means rediscovering our gentleness after a lot of harshness and neglect have made us reactively angry and defensive.

Read and reread this above action plan to become familiar with how to self-regulate using the Gamut Point by tapping, holding, or massaging this back-of-hand area as you practice regulated breathing, feel your feelings, think your thoughts, or speak aloud your trauma stories. By doing so, you will stabilize and deepen your release of the traumatic reactivity stored in the body.

For kinesthetic learners, that is, folks who learn by doing and imitating, arrange to have an introductory session with a trusted professional who uses EFT as well as other techniques to support client healing. Most therapists, coaches, and counsellors offer free consults in which the techniques can be demonstrated quickly and easily. Should you want more support, visit YouTube sites that teach the tapping points but avoid using scripts. Your own words reflecting your personal experiences are always best. If you have an official Diagnostic and Statistical Manual (DSM) diagnosis from a psychiatrist or a clinical psychologist, be sure to ask your mental-health doctor if EFT is right for you.

CLOSING THOUGHTS FOR YOUR RETURN TO WHOLENESS

Generally, treat yourself well: eat nourishing food, drink lots of water, limit screen time, and read and/or listen to inspirational stories about healing after trauma. Watch documentary films about the highs and lows of life of life after trauma and the solidarity we find with other survivors. Whenever you can, go to bed by ten pm in a dark, quiet room. By doing so, you will show your self the love and care and stability we all long for throughout our lives.

Do this wholeness work daily, even if only for fifteen minutes. Include EFT as a vital component of the spiritual food you need to fully experience your wholeness. Record your discoveries in words and images in a journal devoted to your return to wholeness. Get creative. Swear if you need to during EFT sessions when remembering a painful story. Celebrate your ability to let loose and express what you really feel. Wholeness always includes the joy and the sorrow, the rage and the peace we are all capable of feeling.

Remember, returning to wholeness does not involve perfection. Wholeness contains and embraces our best and worst impulses, our potential for kindness and our potential for cruelty. Choosing kindness over cruelty is the work of human maturation, a developmental task we are all called to master and implement. All of the tools and information in this booklet support our maturation into wholeness, into kindness, into compassion and empathy. May you feel supported as you embrace all the parts of your unique, remarkable return to wholeness and the many gifts and challenges your wholeness has for you.

NOTES

NOTES

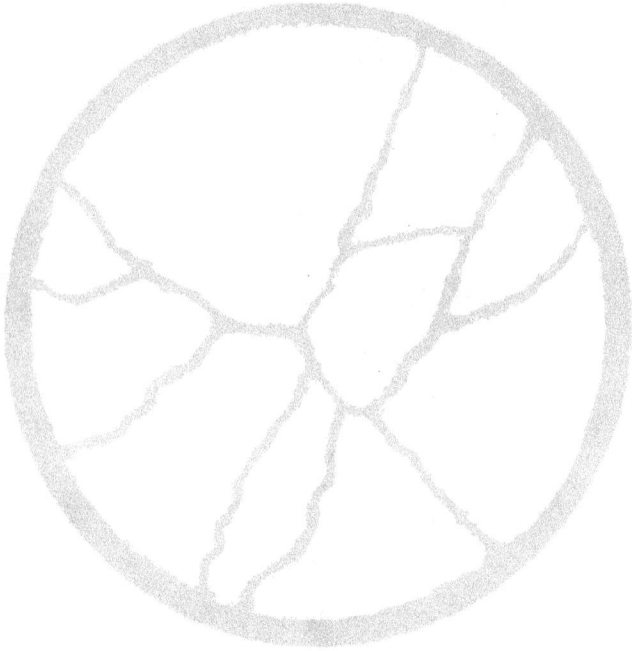

NOTES

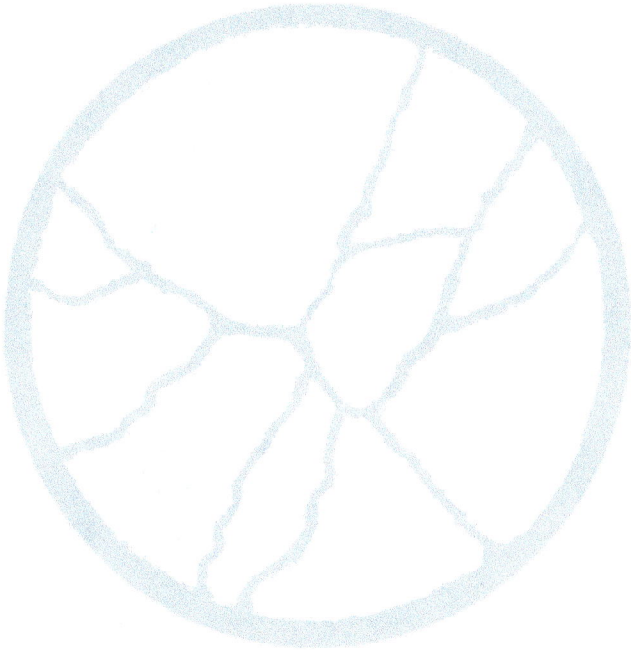

NOTES

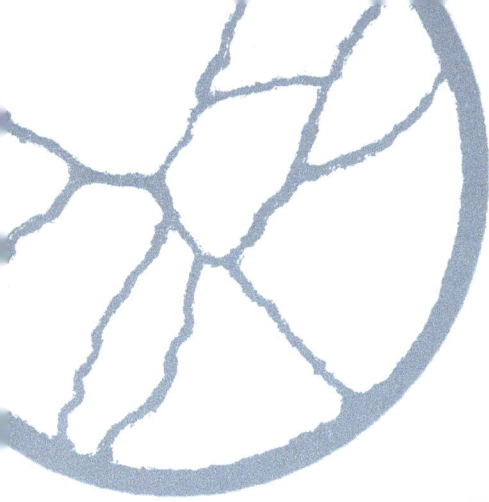

Developmental Trauma: The Igniting Spark

My personal trauma began with a medically required seven-month quarantine in a five-sided crib. Just after my second birthday, our family doctor assured my mother that my stuffy breathing would be cured by a routine tonsillectomy. My left lung collapsed during sedation for this surgery, prompting a search for the cause of my weakened lungs. A chest X-ray revealed my mother's full-blown tuberculosis. My lung collapse and my mother's tuberculosis required immediate isolation from family and one another, I for seven months in a children's TB preventorium, my mother for two years in the TB sanitarium on the same grounds. When I "met" my mother after her two-year quarantine, I no longer remembered her.

My father left our family soon after our quarantine began. With both parents gone and no one else to care for her, my older sister, six at the time, was placed in the care of our maternal grandmother. Widowed at forty-seven two years before our quarantine, she was caring for her elderly mother through the final stages of untreatable cancer. My grandmother's early widowhood, grief and anger over her mother's and her daughter's traumas, and her unexpected parenting role for my sister, and, after seven months, for me, continued to feed our family dysfunctionality throughout my childhood.

Readers interested in a more complete version of my early trauma and later return to wholeness will find it in *Once Upon a Body/Creating Meaning, Peace, and Joy after Early Trauma*, available through Amazon's print-on-demand and digital services.

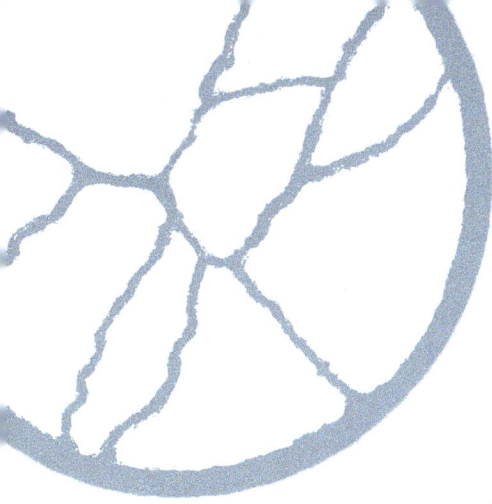

Reflections on Trauma, Identity, Boundaries, and Wholeness

(The original version is available in *Once Upon a Body*, Part II)

Whether we experience trauma in early childhood or in later life, we lose essential connections, to family and friends when we are older, and, whether young or old, to self/Self. As infants and toddlers this lack of connection manifests as profound physical discomfort. When trauma strikes during adolescence and adulthood, we lose a connection to the resourced, confident 'I' we built throughout childhood. Much of my earlier personal work, what I called my Soul-making on my return to wholeness, was about feeling safe enough to connect with others, to put out feelers regarding who 'I' might be in relation to them. When I was young, the only time I did not feel the anxiety of disconnection was when I played in the natural world, enjoyed the pleasures of dance, and explored the realms of story. These intuitive, "bottom up" healing sources soothed my reactive physiology.

Through their positive effects on my nervous system and on the sensory traumas active in my flesh, nature, dance, and story provided an experience of connection to something greater than self/Self. As I now understand these initial sources of intermittent connection, they swept me into non-egoic, joy-inspiring, nourishing flow, what I now know to be wholeness.

As a traumatized child and adolescent, I felt peaceful when the greater-than-human world took me into its tapestries of sound and colour and harmony. Dance, alone and with others, activated my social engagement system for as long as the music lasted. And from my very earliest experiences, story expanded my growing understanding of my own and others' lives before and after quarantine. When I needed a more conscious experience of healing, these personal experiences of wholeness made choosing to enter formal therapy possible. This conscious choice informed all the other forms of formal, "top-down," other-directed healing to come.

Over the decades of my experiences of wholeness, hit and miss as they were, a shift took place, this shift below my conscious awareness. Moving through my life as a person recovering from developmental trauma, with my share of sadness and happiness, work and play, kindness and cruelty, I realized at some point that I no longer sought safety when I felt emotional distress and sensory reactivity. An internal, calm confidence had replaced my autonomic, hypervigilant orientation toward safety, a calm I experienced only rarely when I was younger and vulnerable to what my traumatizing past interpreted as constant, predatory threat.

The source of this deep, centred calm has many moving parts, some of which I suspect I will never be able to name. What I can name is my ability to trust myself in two vital spheres. These spheres are very different but of equal in importance. The first sphere I experience as *knowing who I am*, not in spite of my early trauma and its considerable fallout, but because of it. The second sphere I experience as *holding fast to who I am in the presence of others' distress*. These two spheres became integral to my return to wholeness because the ability to know where I ended and others began was never completely developed during the traumatic circumstances of my childhood. For many years, I lost my bearings in relation to others and to that part of myself I now call 'I' with confidence and clarity. During this time of misplaced identity, I had no sense experience of 'I' as a distinct entity, since I did not know where my 'I' began and ended. The gradual formation of my missing 'I' developed from conscious boundary work.

One of my most important insights during the reclamation of my wholeness involved understanding the extent of what I now call self/Self loss. It took a very long time for me to recognize that my early childhood trauma robbed me of my sense of identity. Before quarantine, knowing who I was, even as a toddler, fueled my strength and vitality and adventurousness. My family relationships provided my toddler identity through their interconnections with me. My parents did their best to comfort me after accidents, set physical boundaries to ensure my safety, and employ all the non-verbal behaviours – smiling, frowning, and cuddling among these – that instill a sense of loving connection.

As I moved through my pre-quarantine days, because of these interactions with my increasingly trusted family members, I experienced my identities as sister, daughter, granddaughter, and niece. I consider myself very fortunate to have had those first two years of deep tissue, sensory experience of self/Self in relation to others in my family. Without them, my ability to recover would have been seriously impacted, for it was during those two pre-quarantine years that I came to know and to trust, first my mother and the comforting, playful experiences I enjoyed with her. My father's building preoccupations gave him a woody scent, one I find comforting to this day. My sister, smaller and far more interesting to me than my parents, became a magnetic force pulling me through those early days of carefree play.

These ordinary yet profoundly vital familial connections were well on their way to creating a flourishing, confident child when our quarantine disaster struck. In a highly roundabout journey of discovery, I learned that losing these relationships schooled me in their importance. I took decades to understand how essential these relationships had been to my recovery once quarantine destroyed my ability to trust anyone, including myself.

What I learned because of that rupture in my ability to trust became the gold at the centre of my new identity. Simply put, my learning went something like this: when we are loved and nurtured, the impatience of an older sibling, the sudden scream of a father's saw, the anxious voice of a mother crying 'no' are but temporary clouds blocking an otherwise sunny existence. They mean little, if noticed at all. Beloved babies and toddlers such as I – in spite of in-utero and birth challenges – are all about learning the powerful 'I' of life. 'I need food. I need comfort. I want food. I want comfort.' And when words come, they are expressive of this supremacy and entitlement. 'Me dat,' sums up the feeling of ruling the world a loved baby develops without any effort at all.

This early, ideal, me-centric way of being in the world works to our advantage by allowing us to form an ego, a sense of self/Self that eventually translates as 'I am I and You are You.' Our awareness of self/Self is awareness of a personal boundary. When all goes well during infancy and toddlerhood, we are socialized gently out of our me-awareness and into the world of you-awareness, and, ultimately, into the ideal we-awareness and behaviours weaving us into healthy interdependent social and community relationships. Bonds broken in infancy and toddlerhood translate as lost ego, lost identity, and lost connection.

The work of healing from trauma for all children and adults disconnected from safety by events beyond our control is to refashion an identity that connects us to self/Self, to others, and to the greater-than-human world in which we are immersed and by whom we are constantly claimed as kin. Reestablishing our vital human connections may not be a simple task, but it is a rewarding one. This rebuilding of identity as an individual separate from others and then as a facet of the vast 'we' of humanity is no less than the lived experience of wholeness.

What I continue to learn from my own and others' identity rebuilding experiences feeds my optimism about our chances of recovery individually and collectively, no matter how devastating the trauma. We need to recover if we are to participate in the larger healing work required by our environmental, social, and political crises. When we consciously do our unique identity-repair work, we build trust in ourselves. Over time, our expanding self-trust supplants our hypervigilant reactivity with a growing capacity for meaning, joy, and optimism. Joyful optimism is the rich fruit of that awareness of wholeness and harmony that began immediately after quarantine in my grandmother's beautiful little garden.

My personal experience of wholeness has depended upon developing through failure after failure my sense of competence, that human characteristic we call self-efficacy. This vitally important, learned character trait has been a key contributor to my transformation from fearful, bewildered, dissociating, adolescent to fully present and trusting adult. Dr. Pat Ogden's explorations of Pierre Janet's acts of completion and triumph helped me to understand why. As a youngster, when I danced, I released some of my unconscious isolation pain through the movement itself, and, equally important, through the mammalian connections dance provided. Reestablishing my sense of community, here a word describing a place I felt I belonged, however fleetingly, ignited the end of my medical-trauma isolation from other people. That I lacked cognitive understanding of what was happening didn't matter. Whenever I danced, I experienced the joy of safe embodiment in the company of others, something I hadn't felt in my grandmother's home nor in my elementary and secondary classrooms, except for my high school senior English classes.

For as long as the dance music lasted, I experienced the healing sensations of reconnection that had nothing to do with my birth family. The faithful physical responsiveness I experienced on the dance floor was the healthiest version of my somatic and emotional reactivity. My physical responses to the rhythms of our adolescent dance rituals along with the opportunity to learn and to replicate steps and patterns, embedded in my flesh the possibility of an autonomous and optimistic adulthood. As well, dance's ability to reunite me with my flesh provided a sensory experience of my physical boundary so necessary to my budding experience of wholeness.

Quarantine literally knocked me off my legs, held me hostage to the relentless protocols of medical procedure, and left me isolated in a tiny, terrifying prison. If ever I needed to rediscover my ability to inhabit my body in a safe and pleasurable way, it was during my teen years when adolescence demands we strengthen our legs and discover our wings. Exercising my right to move through time and space as I danced not only provided pleasure, it restored the authoritative and trustworthy nature of my flesh. One of the only jokes I remember from my high-school dance initiation suggests the innate power of rhythmic physical movement. 'Why do Baptists forbid sex standing up?' The answer still delights me. 'They're afraid it will lead to dancing.'

Dancing, walking, hopping, running, jumping, climbing, and skating support our self-efficacy, the belief that we can accomplish what we set out to accomplish, regardless of the difficulties we meet in pursuit of our goals. Think of toddlers straining to reach a toy on a table. Just newly standing, they stretch up, and up, and fall. Because they have only raw impulse at this stage of development, they repeat this process until they co-ordinate reaching, standing, and grasping in a single, fluid sequence.

This exquisite accomplishment brings joy, and joy is the feeling we experience when we accomplish acts of completion and triumph. However small our early triumphs, they pave the way for the trial-and-error world we inhabit before we hear the unhelpful stories insisting failure must be avoided at all cost. Our baby and toddler triumphs exist within a stage of physical and emotional experimentation that relies on failure as much as success to support the growth of self-efficacy. When we at last accomplish these seemingly inconsequential baby and toddler acts of completion and triumph, we are developing trust in our ability to master new skills and set and achieve new goals, regardless of the difficulties we may encounter. Recovering our self-trust is a vital component of healing after trauma, because self-trust generates the energy of joyful optimism, and joyful optimism makes all the facets of life, even its most trying challenges, facets of our basic wholeness.

When I reflect upon my formal therapy experience, I am grateful that my therapist and I agreed to part two years after we began our work together. My continued relationship with her might well have convinced me that I was incapable of taking action as needed, that our cocoon of safety was the world rather than a temporary respite from the world, a respite in which I might regroup with a wise guide who could support my attempts to understand the sources of emotional pain in my life, at least to that point. Ending our relationship meant that the emotional and spiritual muscles I needed to continue to mature would form when I met my challenges outside of the therapeutic hour, muscles I needed to use then and need to use now to expand my sense of wholeness.

For more than a decade, my early trauma left me without a personal identity and without the conscious knowledge that I would need to create one. Without an identity, I had no idea who 'I' was, what 'I' could do, and who 'I' might become. The only way 'I' could learn about this mysterious self/Self depended upon my full participation in the world, with the possibility of therapeutic support in the background, available as required. My early learning mentors in reconnection – the natural world, dancing, and storytellers, including therapist attachment-and-loss guides – made invaluable differences in my life. Each in their way strengthened the healthy conscious and intuitive activities that contributed to my identity and boundaries. Each trusted me to figure things out – to follow steps, to understand a dramatic arc, to write an academic paper, and to make psychological leaps in understanding – all of which contributed to my identity formation and growing experience of wholeness.

In mothering my children, I discovered yet another source of intuitive healing and sense of identity. As an 'I' and as a 'we,' my mothering self/Self grew into an ever-expanding bond with my children that taught me vital lessons about trust, as a parent and as a person. A slight noise in the night, a shift in breathing, a certain look around the eyes, cued me to respond to my children's needs. I took in the surprises that came each day as spiritual food, watching my daughter's whole-body delight as she tasted her first strawberry and hearing my son mysteriously make truck noises by blowing through his closed lips without any coaching at all, each witnessed act and shared pleasure strengthening our connections to one another. Taking my children to the garden to introduce them to the plants and the trees and the sky, all ordinary, everyday events, supported our growing capacity for love, for each other and for the world.

Observing their play with neighbourhood children in our back garden taught me how they picked up my tones of voice and their father's habits of precision. The more I related to them the more I could discern our influence as well as their unique habits of relationship and solitude. Throughout the years of their childhood, I met my limits of physical energy, discovered a surprising store of courage when they were threatened, and learned that through it all I was also reparenting my neglected child self. All the things taken from me by trauma – stability, familiarity, physical freedom, and safety – returned to me as a mother. During this intense and mostly joyful time, parenting became, even more than dance, my most primal embodying experience. Growing each child in the hidden world of my flesh immersed me in wonder.

Their births called from my flesh the singing and laughing and talking so necessary to mother-child bonding, and our mutual responsiveness became the greatest source of joy I have yet experienced. Parenting also catapulted me into the ferociously protective reactivity of mother bears, lions, and elephants. After defending them against wasps, adult carelessness, or sudden, frightening playground cruelty, I couldn't help but smile at my unapologetic defense of these wonderful beings, and I am grateful that this mammalian, implacable self/Self continues to inform the constantly expanding 'I' of my identity and experience of wholeness.

Teaching also expanded my sense of self/Self in relation to students and colleagues, forming the foundation of my adult, professional identity. Whatever the age level, teaching required I think on my feet, hold the backstory of students in my awareness, and teach to individual needs as well as to curriculum requirements. Some students activated my rescuer impulses, providing opportunities to shore up my boundaries. Some dismissed my views on the value of education and reflection, and their rejections increased my sensitivity to others' journeys and experiences different from my own. Some let me know they felt seen by another person, and that being seen had made a positive difference.

My identity continued to solidify when dancing in community restored my at-homeness in the presence of others when I felt vulnerable. This community dance form also activated another personal characteristic. I am a worshipful creature, one highly responsive to the beauty and harmony of our spiritual interconnectedness as we live out our lives on Earth. This community, circular form of dance brought out this reverent part of my nature, along with the joyful, mischievous kid in me, offering an opportunity to reclaim lost childhood and adolescent experiences through dance camps and the joy of adult play.

My habit of writing, however, remains the most consistent support of my identity-formation process, continually expanding my sense of the 'I' I live from each moment. Early on, academic writing supported my critical thinking skills, an ability sorely lacking until my experiences of emotional resonance with Prince Hamlet in my third year of high school. Yet, as important as it was to learn to craft and prove an argument with critical supports, it was my creative writing process that made my soul leap with fiery joy. *Under the Moon*, my first novel, helped me to express my outrage at the warehousing of vulnerable elders that is caused by the fear of aging at the heart of western culture. That novel's writing process catalyzed my ability to imagine new ways of living together at every age, with spaces for individual privacy and communal life, and with intergenerational, interracial, and intercultural experiences enriching every age and stage of human life.

Because my grandmother raised me, she and her friends expressed the gender experiences of earlier generations, girls and women who were considered the property of boys and men and so had few choices in life. My grandmother and her women friends made up for this early deprivation with a flourishing autonomy in middle and old age. Because of their early traumatic restrictions, these women were passionately determined to experience life to the fullest as they aged. While they experienced aging's inevitable challenges, they did not experience any diminution of spirit. 'I' realized this could be my future as well.

My great aunts were included in this group of fiercely independent older women until a series of tiny strokes ignited a blaze of medical should-and-should-nots that led them to move to a retirement institution. Their experiences of deadening routine and the medicalization of their lives shocked them out of their previous autonomous identities. The contrast between the self-determined people they had been and the dependent people the medical model ensured they would become worked on my heart and mind until Edna Carver, *Under the Moon*'s disgruntled, anti-heroine, took her place at my elbow. From this position, Edna stoked my outrage at the loss of my aunts' individuality and autonomy and seeded my imagination with possibilities of how community living in old age might be different, inclusive, supportive, roomy enough for care as well as the chosen commitments and adventures of older individuals.

No publisher or agent commissioned *Under the Moon*. Only Edna Carver insisted I pay attention, reflect on, and empathize with individuals caught in the toils of the medical establishment's appropriation of the final acts of a long, productive life. Edna Carver's strengths, her prejudices, her fears, absorbed my attention until I told her story and released it into the world. Once McClelland & Stewart published *Under the Moon*, my unhealed trauma, my father's sudden, shocking death, and growing marital difficulties meant that my next novel had to be put on hold.

Throughout that time of emotional challenge and creative writing frustrations, I had my journal. Writing in its pages continued to support my understanding of who 'I' am at my core. It was during this time that I explored how medical expectations and routines cut short my great aunts' autonomy. By doing so, I could imagine my own experiences of lost agency and adventure as a two-year old. As I wrote and reflected and expanded on what I'd written, I came to understand that while my aunts' cage was roomier than mine, and better furnished, their metaphorical prison was stronger because they were victims of the cultural belief in the necessity of removing older adults from the flow of life to ensure their safety. At least my quarantine imprisonment was far from the norm of mainstream experience, and its unusual circumstances meant that I, with others, could address the harm it caused. My aunts had no such support for breaking free.

Once *Under the Moon* was out in the world, I grew more anxious as I moved into a more public life. Now, I am glad of the anxiety I felt after I ended my formal therapy. Had I not experienced that mysterious unease, I wouldn't have sought out the amazing Jungian literature that saw me through times when I most needed their spiritual perspective to navigate my father's shocking death, my failing marriage, and my grandmother's absence from my life. This anxiety also gave me another gift, one 'I' wouldn't understand until I recognized the tools and habits that made it possible to engage my body along with my emotions and thoughts and so deepen my experiences of wholeness.

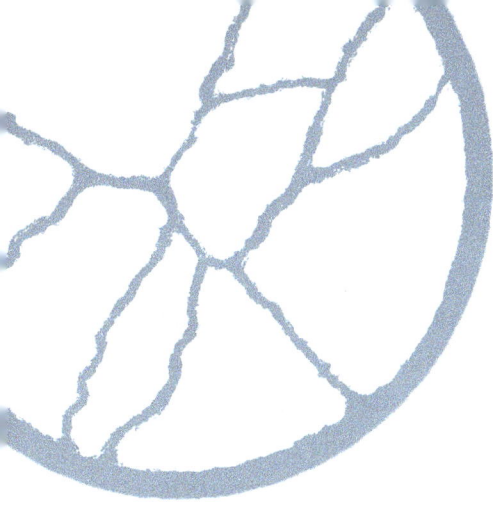

Reflections on Trauma, Toxic Shame, Empowerment, and Wholeness

(The original version is available in *Once Upon a Body*, Part II)

The anxiety I began to feel after the publication of *Under the Moon* (see Appendix Two) marked the beginning of a new awareness of my wholeness, one I wouldn't recognize for several years. This anxiety stemmed from my first-hand experience of toxic shame. By the time I finally understood what generated my post-publication anxiety, my trauma knowledge and general skills provided the ballast I needed to explore how developmental trauma had been influencing my life. By then, thanks to the restorative justice model originating in Indigenous cultures in Australia and Canada, I'd learned to distinguish between two kinds of shame, legitimate and toxic. Most adults suffering from developmental trauma experience both.

Legitimate shame kicks in when we behave as we know we shouldn't, such as bullying a younger sibling, stealing a valued item from a friend, or lying about our part in an act of vandalism and allowing others to take the blame. Legitimate shame dissipates when we do all we can to make things right. The 'Making Amends' step in twelve-step programs is about addressing legitimate shame.

Toxic shame is very different. It is not attached to any specific personal act and so cannot be lessened through any remediating action we might take. Toxic shame becomes a constant, physiological state of dis-ease when others' words and actions frighten and diminish us over a long period of time. Because of the barrage of negativity, we come to believe, not that we have done something wrong, but that we ourselves are wrong. In my experience, toxic shame is birthed when we cannot defend ourselves against others' harmful words and actions.

Toxic shame instills the conviction that others can do what they like with us and to us. No baby, child, soldier, sexually assaulted person, or disaster survivor should experience self-blame and self-loathing for the traumas we experience through violations against our person, and yet we do. 'I should have . . .; If only I'd. . .; Why didn't I . . .? I must be . . ..' These are but few of the opening phrases signaling the presence of reactive, toxic shame.

In infant and toddler non-verbal, sensory language, we feel, sense, and know in our bones we are unloved and unprotected when traumatic experiences are not recognized and remedied quickly. For infants and young children who experience broken attachments, toxic shame's many sensations, along with the beliefs these sensations generate, become more specifically associated with the circumstances of our traumas as we mature. 'I must be worthless,' we unconsciously conclude when we are left to suffer alone, 'if this keeps happening to me.' As we age and learn to articulate our feelings, we find ourselves consciously believing various versions of

'I must be worthless. Why else would they treat me this way? Why else would this have happened to me?' Because of the developmental impact of trauma on our cognitive, intimacy, self-knowledge, and agency skills when we are young, we cannot help but develop the habit of and belief in the self-blame that expresses toxic shame. Toxic shame activates our compulsion to be invisible, to hide, often in plain sight, through dissociation. This physiological reaction to situations in which we feel powerless and disconnected prevents our ability to authentically connect with self/Self and others.

When we are left alone with our traumatic experiences, we assume from our pervasive distress that what has been done to us is permanent and 'how things are.' This is the voice of resignation that leads us to erase ourselves in the attempt to avoid more trauma. When we face our traumas alone, the various situations we experience transform into terrifying unknowns filled with potential predators. Disappearing into a dissociative state, no matter how briefly, numbs the sensations of disconnection, terror, and worthlessness. In spite of our dissociation, toxic shame remains with us, often morphing into rage because of the injustice at the heart of our isolation. This potential for exploding in rage lasts until we are able to recognize and name the burdensome toxic sensations and beliefs we carry, understand their many sources, and grieve them. When the grieving process has done its work, we have integrated these energies into our expanding sense of wholeness, a feeling state that includes the joy generated by acts of completion and triumph, including grieving and integration.

On my personal return to wholeness, toxic shame revealed itself as one of the most debilitating consequences of my unhealed trauma. Before I knew how to recognize and name it, identify its sources, and, eventually, grieve and integrate it, toxic shame prompted me to seek out therapy. This shame lived on the surface of my skin and deep within my organs. It played havoc with my nervous system and made ordinary events such as social gatherings cruel and isolating. Its messages were always icily factual. In spite of my happiness as a mother, a teacher, a writer, and a wife, I would always be broken and therefore, unlovable. At the time I began my formal therapy process, I believed I was to blame for this isolation from others and even for the breakup of my birth family.

Toxic shame tormented me so relentlessly, and embedded its messages so thoroughly in my body, that I believed I was worthless. I slid in and out of this terrible self-rejection until I began formal therapy. Although I felt much better after learning about attachment theory and my personal attachment wounds, I didn't name and understand toxic shame during this therapeutic process because this kind of shame had not yet become a mainstream concept. In the same way that PTSD was named in 1980 and yet took several years for people to understand and identify the links between past trauma and present reactivity, toxic shame wasn't on our cultural radar, at least for people outside of academic research, until John Bradshaw began his televised campaign on behalf of inner-child work in the mid nineteen-eighties.

Although Bradshaw made several effective presentations on PBS, the scientific establishment dismissed his work's importance because its roots sprouted from his own experiences as an abused child in an alcoholic family. I didn't relate to his work since no one in my family abused alcohol or other substances, with the exception of tobacco. Nor had experts yet made clear toxic shame's relationship to abandonment trauma.

When I concluded my formal therapy, I believed I'd solved the problem of feeling worthless and disconnected because of learning about the negative impact of isolation during quarantine. I couldn't include my grandmother's violence against me in this learning because I wasn't yet conscious of its importance. The intellectual knowledge I gained about abandonment and loss created the false belief that my future would be unmarred by that early experience. Back then, once I consciously connected an event to my feelings – such as fear of doctors – I naively believed the issue would disappear. Conversations with my family members about our collective and individual experiences of trauma, along with our authentic expressions of regret, led me to think I'd be free to live my life without my earlier emotional reactivity. This was not the case.

Eventually, I came to understand that my deep well of toxic shame bubbled over during the short promotional book tour to publicize *Under the Moon*. At the time, I had no name for my distress beyond what I laughingly called 'Jane's neurosis.' Unfortunately, my laughing defense didn't dissolve my anxiety. In fact, as the time grew near to leave on my book tour, my inability to sleep through the night returned, along with a serious lack of appetite.

For years afterward, I attributed this period of unmistakable anxiety to leaving my children overnight for the first time. And yet I knew I had no reason to feel worried. Their father was wonderful with them, and I would be away for less than a week. During this time, I called every morning and evening. I knew from these calls that the anxiety our separation caused was entirely on my side. I had no clear idea of its source.

By contrast, my experience of in-the-moment adult fear had a specific reference; losing sight of my children at the playground, being threatened by a stray dog, or feeling endangered by speeding traffic while driving were readily identifiable fears that came and went without leaving emotional residue. The anxiety I felt before the book tour began was very different in that it lacked a clear referent. Because I had no choice in the matter once *Under the Moon* tour dates were set, I lived with this anxiety, pushing through the interviews and comforting myself with the highly plausible stage-fright explanations I'd heard from others doing similar work in the public eye. Fortunately, because of my formal therapy experiences, I had developed the habit of curiosity about my feeling states, exploring these in my daily journal writing. As my anxiety persisted and even deepened in spite of interview successes, I became increasingly interested in understanding why I felt so anxious. I did this through an informal process of elimination.

Since I'd already participated in a number of book talks, I was confident in my responsiveness to readers' questions. By then, because of my teaching commitments, I'd had my share of public speaking experiences that were pleasurable. My subject matter also made speaking engagements highly positive. Exposing the evils of warehousing the elderly through *Under the Moon*'s characters and themes was a cause close to my heart, and I was realistic about the defensive, negative reception this subject matter might provoke. I knew my novel's focus – exploitation of elders – would be difficult for many people. I also understood that awareness of the negative attitudes toward elders had not yet become a mainstream preoccupation and that relatively few people shared my discoveries of neglect and abuse in unsafe, badly run long-term care homes.

In spite of my topic's lack of popularity, I believed in the importance of spreading awareness regarding the crisis-of-care vulnerable elders faced, and I willingly undertook the work of spreading the word about care-facility dangers. I was also confident that the on-the-ground research I did for my great aunts into retirement and nursing homes in Toronto rooted me in verifiable information about retirement- and nursing-home conditions. I was well informed on this topic despite being in my thirties and far from personally facing the spectre of ageism and the powerful seduction of advertisements promoting the benefits of medical-care-focused retirement living. I also had my secret weapons, the example of my grandmother, lively and entirely autonomous as she navigated her early eighties, along with my own quarantine institutionalization war wounds, these personal experiences feeding my passion and very much on my mind thanks to the two years of formal therapy I'd recently concluded.

As well, I had the example of my great aunts' experiences to further strengthen my arguments. A series of small strokes ended one of these aunt's frequent travel adventures, her former autonomy replaced by fear in spite of her quick return to physical health. Before this calamity, my grandmother and her sisters-in-law regularly traveled the four-hundred kilometers separating their homes to visit several times a year. During the winter season their greatest pleasure involved watching 'Hockey Night in Canada' on Saturday evenings while they reminisced about their personal glory days on the ice in Stratford, Ontario. Because we'd all witnessed these three women living adventurous lives well into old age, the undeniable contrast of my great aunts' retirement-home experiences became an important topic of conversation in our family.

As the only member of our family in Toronto, I shared special lunch outings and ran errands for them, keeping my Windsor relatives, anxious on their behalf, informed of their circumstances. Synchronously, the teaching assignment I found when I left the PhD program at York University was only a block away from the retirement home my greats aunts chose to move to after the younger aunt's minor strokes. This close proximity meant I could eat lunch with them at the retirement home at least once a week. Because of our close relationship, I couldn't deny my aunts' shockingly swift shift from independence to fear-based medical preoccupations. Because of what I'd learned about retirement- and nursing-home inadequacies when researching

Toronto homes for them, I was convinced that my book-tour anxiety had nothing to do with feeling ill-prepared to speak out against the practice of over-medicalizing the aging process.

Another telling fact about my anxiety was its persistence. Once home from these publishing duties and returned to my normal routines, my sleeplessness and loss of appetite continued. Throughout this period, my morning journal work focused on what might be going on, but without any breakthroughs. Over time, I learned to live with this constant anxiety, attributing it to having the regular concerns that come with parenting young children, living in a world increasingly violent and unjust, and feeling helpless in the face of growing emotional disconnection from my husband.

It was not until I learned Gary Craig's Emotional Freedom Techniques to support my mother's dying process more than twenty years after the onset of this anxious period that I found a safe way to explore why this anxiety had blossomed when McClelland & Stewart published *Under the Moon*. By the time I learned EFT, I'd heard many lectures on toxic shame, some by John Bradshaw, some by experts in inner-child work, but I'd never applied this information to my personal experiences. My awareness shifted when I began to use Craig's Personal Peace Procedure.

As I tapped on various hot-button memories and beliefs, space for further exploration grew around what I'd so glibly called 'Jane's neurosis.' During work on many of my ongoing conscious memories of this anxious period in my life, several images arose from my unconscious. One of these, an image of me as a toddler in a cage during quarantine, caused me to weep as I'd wept during my first few months of dancing in community. These tears for my toddler self surprised me because most images that surfaced precipitated anger and even rage. As I wept, I tapped, focusing on the image of the caged toddler I'd been. I soon discovered the reason for my tears. The young child I had been felt utterly lost, 'disappeared out of existence,' a feeling I'd been unaware of before that tapping session. Learning that I felt 'disappeared out of existence' as a very young child turned out to be a transforming discovery.

From that moment on, I used Craig's tapping sequences to address feeling unworthy of existence. My inability to escape my cage, I realized as I tapped, had given birth to my version of toxic shame. At long last I understood a core belief: *being caged for seven months made me feel 'I' didn't deserve to live.* My lifelong desire to hide in certain situations, to become invisible, along with the reactive terrors that disappeared me into dissociative states suddenly make sense.

As I tapped on 'my need to hide,' I gained insight into the long-term effects of my quarantine experiences and their relationship to the period of anxiety before, during, and after the *Under the Moon* book tour. These insights led me deep into the sensory residue of caged isolation. While the medical protocols of the time were intended to return me to health, they exposed my body to strangers' scrutiny throughout each day and night. Although I wouldn't have the caged feelings of worthlessness to compare with my interview experience for a very long time, once I gained access to the experiences of my young caged self, I sensed how my toddler body felt pinned to a blotter – an image that first came to me during my interviews for *Under the Moon*. During those interviews, through no fault of the people involved, I often felt the same sensations of being under merciless scrutiny, skewered by a pin and helplessly flapping my wings in the attempt to escape.

Throughout the seven months I spent in quarantine, I'd been entirely at the mercy of well-meaning people who objectified me as they performed the procedures they were trained to administer. These procedures had two goals. The first was to strengthen my lungs after my exposure to my mother's full-blown tuberculosis. The second was to prevent risk of spreading tuberculosis in our community. As I worked through the feelings and sensations attached to this early time, I came to realize that being in front of cameras when in my thirties on the book tour had triggered the quarantine sensations and feelings of objectification that began when I was two. At the time of my book tour, my knowledge of John Bowlby's Attachment Theory was intellectual. This intellectual understanding couldn't prevent my anxiety because this feeling state had been generated by my physical store of traumatizing sensations.

My unhealed sensory trauma initiated an entirely reactive cascade of physical-threat sensations my intellect might eventually understand but could not prevent. I couldn't consciously connect my deep tissue store of toxic shame to my early medical trauma and its emotional legacy because I hadn't yet learned the concept. Even if my therapist and I had been able to discuss toxic shame, my time with her did not address my somatic reactivity, except when talking about uncontrollable laughing and compulsive climbing as safety valves.

Throughout the eighties, my academic knowledge, therapy discoveries, and general resourcefulness supported my participation as an interviewee on book tours and as a teaching applicant, while my body, constantly animated by my unhealed somatic reactivity, felt unsafe. I wouldn't make this connection between the two very different experiences of knowledge – intellectual and physical/emotional/intuitive – until I recognized and began to use Craig's simple techniques to address the shame that had lodged in my flesh when I was continuously handled by strangers trained to objectify me as they efficiently executed the required medical procedures.

My personal cache of toxic shame remained entirely visceral until well into my fifties despite being conscious of an irrational desire to hide in certain situations. I was aware, for example, of a powerful withdrawal impulse in certain social situations that were disconnected from professional duties. For many years, I attributed this hiding impulse to my introversion. Eventually, I admitted that my introversion never prevented me from socializing in relation to my professional duties where my role as teacher was clear and the ambiguity of purely social events absent. Once I began using body-inclusive techniques to focus on the experiences of toxic-shame reactivity still active in my body, I realized I had been using my professional expertise to block this sensory reactivity. When I didn't have this professional protection, I felt anxious to the point of dissociating to feel safe, at least on a somatic level.

During my Personal Peace Procedure work, I finally understood these withdrawal impulses as attempts to restore a sense of equilibrium whenever I felt threatened. Once I connected my early experiences of objectification to toxic-shame reactivity everything changed.

I understood this 'worthless,' disappeared-out-of-existence reactivity as my two-year old's only means of registering my experiences. In quarantine, because of the objectivity of carers, I experienced very real versions of predation although no one intended for me to have this experience. When I finally understood the reasons for my compulsion to hide, I tapped on my grief, my rage, and my loss of the preventorium doctor's kindness. As I did, my impulses to withdraw and to hide ebbed away.

I also learned that in the 1940s and in present-day medical practices, patient objectification is one of the downsides of medical treatment. Covid 19 protocols are a vivid case in point. When dealing with contagious diseases, isolation is considered both cure and prevention, and while quarantine may be the best option in certain circumstances, the harm caused by enforced isolation grows when it is not acknowledged and actively addressed. I am remembering poignant images of family members visiting elders at picture windows, their hands pressed together with glass preventing actual touch.

For the family members who feel helpless because their older relatives are suddenly isolated and afraid, the risk of toxic shame is high. Self-blame grows out of protracted feelings of helplessness to alter circumstances. This is affecting families with elders in nursing homes, families with loved ones in ICUs, and families with adolescents and young children whose ordinary lives have been restricted by isolation protocols. While the protocols are enforced to prevent spread of the disease, I have no doubt that the next development in quarantine treatment will be to create emotional support to acknowledge and to heal the consequences of sudden, absolute separation and loss. This next step will help to prevent the development of toxic shame in the isolated as well as in their family members and professional care providers.

The separation of children from parents and other family members that occurred at the US-Mexican border is another example of isolation that leads to toxic shame, in the parents, in the children, and in their jailors. I suspect that parents and jailors who were unable to prevent such separations felt and continue to feel the heartlessness behind the abusive policy and consciously or unconsciously blame themselves for not being able to prevent such abuse. Children separated from their family members feel the terror of being inhumanly caged and abandoned, their bodies learning the sensory horror that translates as, 'No one wants me. I've lost everything. I must be worthless.' It is not enough to reunite families after such politically orchestrated assaults on vital human relationships. Family members and entire communities are needed to consciously work to return to wholeness after such terrifying experiences.

When I lost my relationships with my family members and my familiar surroundings, I experienced the end of my carefree, secure life as a loved child. As soon as I entered the hospital for a routine tonsillectomy, I became an object, one controlled by unfamiliar, sometimes insensitive hands, not because people were intentionally cruel, but because our understanding of children's needs and sensitivities were then in their infancy. All my small gains of autonomy as a two-year-old vanished the moment a nurse took me howling from my mother's arms. Once held captive within the preventorium, I could not use the toilet. I could not ask my mother for water or toast. I could not play fetch with my dog. I could not dance to the records I played on my record player. I could not move through my familiar surroundings as I pleased. Worst of all, I did not have the cognitive development to understand why my sudden imprisonment happened. In the chaotic soup that is abandonment trauma, my sense of betrayal and rage must have been enormous. Unlike my empowered toddler life at home, in both the hospital and preventorium I was impotent. I could not alter a single detail of my experience.

The experience of impotence and vulnerability is the moment when inexpressible rage goes underground and toxic shame infuses the body's bones, muscles, and blood. My flesh understood this experience as *my* failure – to get away, to summon a parent. As I grew older and my cognitive development re-ignited, the story in my flesh reflected my new understanding, and my reasoning went something like this: 'all that happened to me is my fault, and so I must be very bad; 'I' – my very *self* – must be shameful, unworthy, and undeserving of all comfort.'

Before my quarantine, whenever I needed to, I could express outrage at not getting what I wanted. I could lie on the floor, kicking and screaming until 'I' made something happen. I could find my special blanket and curl up with it for comfort. I could cuddle with my dog. I could go to my mother and ask to be held. Quarantine provided none of the opportunities for agency that guaranteed comfort in my previous life. Locked within an unfamiliar, sterile institution, I was a literal prisoner, already deep in the immobilizing, dissociative state that renders a temper tantrum impossible.

In his research into how the Polyvagal System works, Stephen Porges discovered that the dissociative state is governed by the oldest part of our autonomic nervous system. This primal defense mechanism, popularly known as the freeze response, is activated by trauma. The dorsal vagus nerve's protective cocoon of immobility, the one we witness when an animal goes limp under predator threat, kicks in when struggle is futile. In this state of dorsal-vagal dissociation, the 'I' of my previous life not only shut down, it felt shamed out of existence. Discovering how toxic shame made me want to hide, a discovery made through daily attention over the days and weeks and months of my early experimentation with a variety of techniques that engaged my body, my mind, and my heart, remains one of my most empowering experiences of wholeness.

When I first began to use the tools of self-regulated breathing, writing, and tapping, toxic shame had been activating my impulse to hide for more than five decades. Eden Energy Medicine and Emotional Freedom Techniques became my go-to exploratory tools, because I could experiment with them on my own, a factor that contributed to my growing sense of safety and agency in the larger world. As good as all the intuitive, body-centred activities had been in supporting my physical release of grief and fear and even rage, including time in the natural world, dancing, and storytelling, these didn't reduce the toxic shame encoded in my flesh because it wasn't active when I was immersed in these healing modalities. Energy tools were different.

Using energy tools to consciously engage the active sensations of worthlessness allowed me to address toxic shame directly, as reactive sensation, defensive impulse, and even terror, all of which triggered my impulse to hide. In my energy-tool sessions, I didn't have to connect toxic shame to an event, because it is a sensory state rather than a memory, a feeling rather than an experience. Most important, I could do this work privately, without triggering the automatic fear of predators, not, in my case, lions or tigers, but the imprisoning authorities of my quarantine. As it turned out, the safety afforded by my ability to work alone on the feelings and sensations stored in my flesh was essential to tuning into the beliefs these sensations activated.

For example, I could simply tap on 'these feelings of shame, these sensations, these impulses that make me want to hide' and experience immediate relief. Despite feeling better almost instantly, once I undertook this energy work to address toxic shame, I continued to use the techniques in this specific way for months. And then, one memorable day, I caught myself in the act of enjoying an impromptu social event with real pleasure. My impulse to hide was nowhere to be found. As I explored this feeling of social ease, I discovered the impulse to hide had transformed into a tender empathy for my and others' suffering, especially when we are most vulnerable and lack the support we depend on for love and care.

Because I continue to use these tools to support my awareness of toxic shame, signs of 'Jane's neurosis' very rarely surface these days. When a sudden feeling of toxic shame does occur, I immediately begin my sleuthing process. In my journal, I acknowledge my discomfort with gentle attention. I also thank my defensive laughter and sense of irony, so frequently my protectors and deflectors during moments of painful vulnerability. As I honour these feelings of terror, helplessness, and rage by attending to the 'worthlessness' narrative prowling around in my flesh, my nervous system calms, my heart slows to its usual steady rhythms, and I get on with my day. The empowerment I feel as I lovingly attend to this sensory traumatic legacy has been my most comprehensive experience of wholeness yet.

My early pain and suffering have connected me to others' suffering through compassion and empathy, more experiences of my wholeness. It has been a challenging process at times, but ultimately, it has been a humanizing one. We are all born whole, and while traumas early and late may obscure our wholeness, our willingness to heal, to integrate our shocks and shakeups by regularly employing these simple awareness tools, leaves us with many more gifts than deficits.

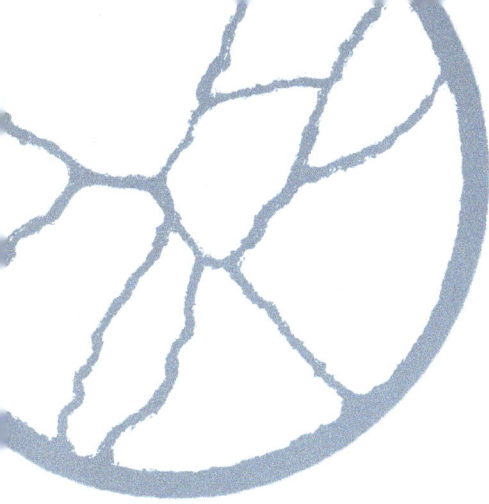

About the Author

Jane Buchan writes about Adverse Childhood Experiences and Adult Trauma from personal and professional perspectives. Her knowledge and experiences have led her to conclude that traumatizing family patterns, educational-system failures, cultural and political divisions, and environmental crises have made trauma-sensitive approaches vital to our personal and collective survival. It is her intention that the tools and reflections in this book, along with her other writings, expand readers' awareness of unresolved traumas' impact on human beliefs and behaviours, and that this awareness fuel personal and collective intentions to evolve into problem solvers capable of living together in cooperative relationships that express our species' wholeness.